Zion's Christian Soldiers? ought to be on the required reading list for all students of the Bible. Here is basic and fundamental methodology that challenges many evangelical assumptions about 'end-times prophecy'. Here is a sound-minded, Christ-centred critique of a popularly accepted, but nonetheless fatally flawed, perspective that leads to many spiritual dysfunctions. If you find yourself troubled by sabre-rattling political rhetoric coming from many pulpits, *Zion's Christian Soldiers?* will reacquaint you with the Prince of peace.
Greg Albrecht, President of Plain Truth Ministries, and Editor-in-Chief, The Plain Truth *magazine*

Thank God, at last here comes a book that challenges the pseudo-theology that, by giving precedence to the old covenant over the new, relegates the church to the status of concubine in order to make Israel the Bride of Christ. In clear and measured terms, the author demonstrates from Scripture that God's purposes for history are not driven by a narrowly selective racist obsession, but rather by his eternal design to create the church, the new community dearly secured through the cross for all Christ-followers, both Jews and Gentiles.
Professor Gilbert Bilezikian, Professor Emeritus, Wheaton College and a founding leader of Willow Creek Community Church, South Barrington, Illinois

In this very readable new work, Anglican vicar Stephen Sizer offers a biblically based interpretation of the relationship of Israel and the Christian church. Turning to the current upsurge of Christian Zionism, Sizer examines its deeply flawed misreadings of key biblical texts and its troubling public-policy implications. Not only Sizer's fellow evangelicals, but everyone interested in this vital topic, will find *Zion's Christian Soldiers?* an illuminating and highly valuable study.
Professor Paul S. Boyer, James Pinckney Harrison Visiting Professor at William and Mary in Williamsburg, Va., and Editor-in-Chief of The Oxford Companion to American History

Few themes in biblical studies
Zionism has brought to the chu
the Bible that future generations
Christian's obligation to understa

GW00492894

should be evaluated. Writing in a style that is accessible to everyone – and with a passion that is sure to ignite strong responses – Sizer outlines the landscape of the problem and its solution.

Professor Gary M. Burge, Professor of New Testament, Department of Biblical and Theological Studies, Wheaton College and Graduate School

I strongly commend this new book by Stephen Sizer and urge all evangelical Christians to read it and consider its warning message. No issue arouses greater confusion and dissent among Christians than Christian Zionism. Even to question its claims draws sharp opposition. Yet none threatens the future of positive Jewish, Christian and Muslim relationships more than Christian Zionism and its connection with the politics of the State of Israel. All too readily, confusing labels and bitter acrimony encourage Christians to leave the issue alone, or to regard it as an intractable political problem that does not concern them. Stephen Sizer has shown the greatest courage in facing its challenges and in providing an informative, irenic and readable exposition of what the issues are and how they have arisen. I urge my fellow Christians to read this book and give it their closest attention.

Professor Ronald E. Clements, Emeritus Professor of Old Testament Studies, King's College, University of London

Stephen Sizer deftly exposes the many exegetical missteps of contemporary Christian Zionists. He advocates a more just and Christ-centred alternative to the politically and ethically problematic views espoused by many contemporary end-times popularizers. I hope this book prompts a courageous and healthy re-thinking of Zionist theology towards a more constructive, biblical perspective.

Dr Paul Copan, Associate Professor and Pledger Family Chair of Philosophy and Ethics, Palm Beach Atlantic University, West Palm Beach, Florida

This work deals expertly with a vital theme. For this Christian zealotry perverts the truth of Christ in three tragic ways. It ignores or repudiates the equal stature under God of all peoples in nature and in grace; it flouts a Christian conscience by discounting injustice and oppression; and it sees no Christian ministry to the hope and pleas of original Zionism itself. Thus, it darkly violates both Christian sympathy and Christian faith.

The Right Reverend Kenneth Cragg, retired Assistant Bishop in Jerusalem

In this seminal work based on a careful analysis of how the Bible explains the relationship between Israel and the church, Stephen Sizer underscores crucial distinctions between anti-Semitism and anti-Zionism. Just as it is a grievous sin to turn a blind eye to the horrors of anti-Semitism, so it is a grievous sin to turn a blind eye to a Zionist theology that divides people on the basis of race rather than uniting them on the basis of righteousness, justice and equity.

Hank Hanegraaff, President of the Christian Research Institute and host of the Bible Answer Man *broadcast*

This subject deeply impacts the Western world and the so-called 'clash of civilizations'. This book is a 'must' for all those concerned about this vital subject.

The Very Reverend Michael Harper, Dean of the British Antiochian Orthodox Deanery and a director of The Institute for Orthodox Christian Studies, Wesley House, Cambridge

This is a clarion call to evangelical Christians to study the Bible more carefully because of the political implications of their beliefs. Stephen Sizer shows that many Christians are espousing views that they claim come from the Bible, but which are in fact leading to bloodshed, dispossession and division in the Middle East. Stephen calls for a more careful look at the Bible that reflects the call of Jesus to be peacemakers.

Garth Hewitt, Founder and International Director of the Amos Trust

A workmanlike study that confronts many treasured and traditional opinions with frankness and sensitivity. An added bonus is the Stott sermon, hitherto unpublished, a masterpiece of clarity in an area marked too often by confusion and unjustified assertions.

Prebendary Dick Lucas, Chairman of the Proclamation Trust and Rector Emeritus of St Helen's, Bishopsgate, London

This much-needed volume, by a well-known evangelical Christian writer, focuses our attention on contested issues in the Holy Land.

Refreshingly, Sizer interprets Scripture from a standpoint of peace and justice rather than of apocalyptic fantasies.

Dr Duncan Macpherson, Honorary Research Fellow at the University of Wales, Lampeter

How should Christians respond to the cascade of prophecy literature flowing from the pens of Hal Lindsey, John Walvoord, Tim La Haye, John Hagee, and others, who claim the Bible itself as authorization for Christian Zionism in all its forms and goals? Probably it is high time to stop regarding their overliteral misinterpretations as the curiosities they are and awaken to the fact that they are also *very dangerous* misreadings of prophecy passages in Scripture, which could lead to catastrophic conflict in the Near East. To help Christians become the peacemakers they ought to be, rather than firebrands inflaming the world with wrongheaded ideas about the end times, Stephen Sizer's new book, *Zion's Christian Soldiers?*, is an ever-so-necessary antidote to the present prophecy mania. With crystal logic and gifted pen, he dismantles the often-grotesque claims made by prophecy specialists and restores sanity to the discussion.

Professor Paul L. Maier, Russell H. Seibert Professor of Ancient History in the Department of History, College of Arts and Sciences, Western Michigan University, Kalamazoo and Vice-President of the Lutheran Church Missouri Synod

This book is an eye-opener to the muddled but militant attitudes among modern evangelicals (particularly Americans) toward the State of Israel. Sizer reveals not only the highly questionable exegeses of Christian Zionism, but also the movement's alarming political agenda and its fallout in our war-torn world. This is a book that every thoughtful evangelical should read.

Bruce A. McDonald, Assistant Professor of Religion, Texas Wesleyan University, Fort Worth, Texas

Stephen Sizer's book, *Zion's Christian Soldiers?*, is a powerful, easily readable, theological refutation of Christian Zionism. In his analysis, Sizer destroys the major arguments of Christian Zionist advocates by primarily citing and interpreting Old and New Testament passages. Although especially valuable reading for evangelical Christians, this book deserves careful study by all people interested in the role played by religion in the Arab–Israeli conflict.

Professor Norton Mezvinsky, Professor of History, Central Connecticut State University

Sizer hits another home run! His treatment of the kingdom of God as both present and transcendent points the believer to the future – not the past.

Dr Stan Moody, Baptist minister and founder of the Christian Policy Institute, www.christianpolicyinstitute.org

This book makes important matters of faith, world and God accessible. For it is far more than a book about Christian Zionism. It is a brave challenge to powerful voices. It raises essential questions of how a Christian is to engage with the world as it focuses on what is happening in Israel and the Occupied Territories, and it is a model in careful, Christ-centred Bible study. It is also a call to prayer, since it focuses upon the most crucial area of Christian in-fighting that at present weakens our witness to the Lord. In addition, it reminds us of the needs of the suffering church and people who are held in the grip of political intransigence.

Revd John Rackley, President of the Baptist Union 2003–4 and Minister of Manvers Street Baptist Church, Bath

Stephen is a faithful minister of the Bible where it concerns Bible prophecy and the modern nation-state of Israel. I remember that when I began studying the second intifada in 2001, finding Stephen's website was like finding buried treasure! In one spot, I stumbled upon every reasonable biblical argument against dispensational Christian Zionism one could need! *Zion's Christian Soldiers?* will offer simple and straightforward answers to the major assertions of noted Christian Zionist leaders from a thoroughly evangelical reading of the Bible. Sizer carefully engages American popular figures such as Hal Lindsey and John Hagee, who are influencing millions of evangelicals into doomsday celebrations. He unpacks in patient detail the heart of the Scriptures that Christian Zionists ignore. I am so very thankful for this kindly teacher. In a day and age in which cynicism, hate, impatient rhetoric, and stewing resentment mark our conversations on this topic, Stephen Sizer is able to speak the simple truth. Would to God that many hear and receive this very timely message.

Chris Rice, Writer and Editor, Jesus People USA, Chicago

Confused about whether Christians should support the State of Israel? Agonizing over the desperate situation in the Middle East today? Stephen Sizer challenges the views that are fashionable in Christian circles, and helps us get to grips with the key issues and understand what the Bible really has to say. A very important contribution to a crucial issue.

Canon John Salter, Vice-Chairman of the Garden Tomb Association and member of the Oak Hill College Council

There was a time when Christians believed that the earth was the centre of the universe. It was not only an error in science but also false church doctrine lasting long after Copernicus and grasping the hearts and minds of Christian literalists who sanctioned punishment and even death for proponents of a larger view of faith and the universe. The history of Christianity is not lacking in false ideas that enjoy popularity for a time then fade under pressure of reason, knowledge and experience. Revd Sizer exposes a modern version of serious religious error in *Zion's Christian Soldiers?*, focusing on the tenets of a dangerous biblical literalism whose vision of God is nationalistic in its bizarre loyalty to the Jewish State of Israel and militaristic in its enthusiastic anticipation of a literal Armageddon. This is an important book for theologians and peacemakers.

The Revd Canon Richard K. Toll, Chair, Friends of Sabeel – North America

A timely and important book. Controversial but persuasive, it deserves to be read by everyone who is prepared to think afresh about God's purposes for the church, Israel and the politics of the Middle East.

Dr Stephen Travis, former Vice-Principal, St John's College, Nottingham

Stephen Sizer's thorough research, theological analysis, and historical contextualization make this volume the 'go to' book on the topic of Christian Zionism. As Christian Zionism continues to grow within Western evangelical churches and para-church agencies, we are reminded that it is now a significant political force in shaping US policy in the Middle East. Additionally, its global reach through satellite broadcasting and the internet adds another significant challenge to Christian missions. Now the gospel of Jesus Christ is represented in a militant, Crusader, Western Zionist construction that is not only hostile to Muslims and Arabs, but is an utter contradiction to the message of love, reconciliation, and good news to the poor and marginalized, whatever their economic status, political orientation, race or creed. After studying this volume and utilizing resources at www.christianzionism.org, you will be better equipped to challenge the false gospel of Christian Zionism.

Professor Don Wagner, Professor of Religion and Middle Eastern Studies, Executive Director: Center for Middle Eastern Studies; Director: The Institute for Christianity, Faith and Culture; North Park University, Chicago

In a challenging and fraught field, Stephen Sizer has provided an excellent, incisive and insightful assessment of the Christian Zionist movement. He precisely and accurately identifies the methods of biblical interpretation that support this damaging group, and indicates how the Bible can be more convincingly interpreted. With a collection of clear and helpful diagrams, he illustrates a far more coherent understanding of the biblical message. He writes clearly and precisely in a style that is easily accessible and readily understandable.

Dr John Wilks, Director of Open Learning, The London School of Theology, London

ZION'S CHRISTIAN SOLDIERS?

To Joanna,
Rachel, Katie, Louise & Michael

ivp

Stephen Sizer

ZION'S CHRISTIAN SOLDIERS?

The Bible, Israel and the Church

Inter-Varsity Press
Norton Street, Nottingham NG7 3HR, England
Email: ivp@ivpbooks.com
Website: www.ivpbooks.com

First published 2007
Reprinted 2008

British Library Cataloguing in Publication Data
A catalogue record for this book is available from the British Library.

ISBN: 978-1-84474-214-1

Set in Monotype Dante 10.5/13pt
Typeset in Great Britain by CRB Associates, Reepham, Norfolk
Printed and bound in Great Britain by Ashford Colour Press Ltd, Gosport,
Hampshire

Inter-Varsity Press publishes Christian books that are true to the Bible and that
communicate the gospel, develop discipleship and strengthen the church for its
mission in the world.

Inter-Varsity Press is closely linked with the Universities and Colleges Christian
Fellowship, a student movement connecting Christian Unions in universities
and colleges throughout Great Britain, and a member movement of the
International Fellowship of Evangelical Students. Website: www.uccf.org.uk

Contents

Preface

Whether you have been recommended this book or have just picked it up out of curiosity, I've probably got only another thirty seconds to convince you to read it. So let me ask you this question: What subject do Christians find most controversial? Abortion? Sex? Climate change? The correct answer is probably *Israel*. No other subject ignites such strong emotions.

A large proportion of Bible-believing Christians are convinced that God blesses those nations that stand with Israel and curses those that don't. This movement, known as Christian Zionism, provides a biblical justification for US intervention in the Middle East. It is deeply mistrustful of the United Nations and the European Community and actively opposes the implementation of international law and the right of Palestinians to a sovereign state alongside Israel.

It is my contention that this world-view is not shaped by the Bible. As a young Christian, I was raised on books like the *Scofield Reference Bible*[1] and Hal Lindsey's *The Late Great Planet Earth*.[2] It took me a while to appreciate that the theology these books assume has radical implications for how we view our faith and the world we live in. The church in Palestine is close to extinction. Jewish Zionism, militant Islam and Christian indifference exacerbate it, but Christian Zionism probably has a greater detrimental effect than the other three causes combined.

Ten years ago, apart from Colin Chapman's *Whose Promised Land?*,[3] Gary Burge's *Who Are God's People in the Middle East?*,[4] Grace Halsell's

Forcing God's Hand[5] and Donald Wagner's *Anxious for Armageddon*,[6] no other evangelicals seemed bold enough to tackle the subject. It is still largely uncharted territory, and that is why I published *Christian Zionism: Road-map to Armageddon?*[7] When IVP invited me to write a second book for a wider readership, I needed no convincing.

Writing this book has got me into a lot of hot water and made me a few enemies along the way. Type my name into Google and you will soon discover who they are. It has also been a lonely journey; there are few evangelicals, it seems, who are willing to challenge the assumption that Bible-believing Christians will automatically support Israel. Why is that? The fear of being labelled 'anti-Semitic' is a powerful disincentive. The power of the pro-Israeli, Christian Right in the USA is very strong and opposes anyone who criticizes Israel or defends the Palestinians. Christian publishers are boycotted, sponsorship for academic institutions is denied and subscriptions to Christian journals are cancelled.

The battle over intellectual freedom is waged in universities on both sides of the Atlantic. Organizations such as Campus Watch[8] and the Union of Jewish Students monitor staff and students and put pressure on the authorities to censure them. Jewish Voice for Peace (JVP) has sought to counter this pressure through their own website. Called rather appropriately, Muzzlewatch,[9] JVP exposes efforts (written and verbal) to prevent open debate about US-Israeli foreign policy. Not surprisingly, they have come under severe attack in the US for doing this.

There are plenty of books that examine 'Zionism' and 'Bible prophecy'. There are few, however, that explain the relationship between the two from a biblical perspective. This one does. My hope is that it will also encourage dialogue on the relationship between Israel and the church, and offer a more constructive view of the future and our role in it.

I need to thank some very special people without whom this book would never have seen the light of day: Philip Duce, Theological Books Editor at IVP, who held me to my promise with words of encouragement and wisdom; Pam Gardiner, who has kindly reworked many of my obtuse sentences into something worth reading; and Alison Hull, who had the vision for this book many years ago and wouldn't give up even when I wanted to.

I owe a deep debt of gratitude to a handful of writers who have had the courage to address aspects of this subject and from whom I have learnt so much. They include Don Wagner, Gary Burge, Colin Chapman, Peter Walker, Gilbert Bilezikian, Naim Ateek, Timothy Weber, John Stott, Gary DeMar, Hank Hanegraaff and Garth Hewitt.

Finally, I want to thank John Stott for his inspiration and leadership, and for an unpublished sermon included here, entitled 'The Place of Israel', which he preached in London many years ago. We have indeed saved the best till last.

All the best material has been borrowed from these people. I gladly accept responsibility for the rest.

Stephen Sizer
Ash Wednesday 2007

1. Introduction: For the love of Zion

Brothers and sisters, my heart's desire and prayer to God for the Israelites is that they may be saved. For I can testify about them that they are zealous for God, but their zeal is not based on knowledge. (Romans 10:1–2)

Unanswered questions?

Why is there such a close relationship today between the Christian Right, the American political establishment and the State of Israel? Why, after forty years, does Israel continue to occupy territory in Lebanon (the Sheba Farms), Syria (the Golan Heights) and Palestine (the West Bank), while Syria has been pressured to withdraw from Lebanon? Why is Israel allowed to retain nuclear weapons, while Iran is threatened with a pre-emptive attack for aspiring to obtain nuclear technology? And how have Britain and America become the focus of so much hate in the Arab world and the target for Islamic terrorism, despite our commitment to the rule of international law, democracy and human rights?

The answers to these questions remain inexplicable unless we factor in what is now probably the most influential and controversial movement amongst Christians today – Christian Zionism.

The significance of Christian Zionism

Let me give you a flavour of the movement and its strategy from a recent speech given by John Hagee. Hagee is the founder and senior pastor of Cornerstone Church, an 18,000-member evangelical church in San Antonio in Texas. Hagee broadcasts a national radio and television ministry to Americans on 160 TV stations, fifty radio stations and eight networks into an estimated 99 million homes worldwide on a weekly basis. In 2006, he founded Christians United for Israel with the support of 400 other Christian leaders.

> For 25 almost 26 years now, I have been pounding the evangelical community over television. The Bible is a very pro-Israel book. If a Christian admits 'I believe the Bible,' I can make him a pro-Israel supporter or they will have to denounce their faith. So I have the Christians over a barrel, you might say.[1]

The assumption Hagee makes, that Bible-believing Christians will be pro-Israel, is the dominant view among evangelical Christians, especially in the USA. In March 2007, Hagee was a guest speaker at the American Israel Public Affairs Committee (AIPAC) Policy Conference. He began with these words: 'The sleeping giant of Christian Zionism has awakened. There are 50 million Christians standing up and applauding the State of Israel . . . '

As *The Jerusalem Post* pointed out, his speech did not lack clarity. He went on to warn:

> It is 1938. Iran is Germany, and Ahmadinejad is the new Hitler.
> We must stop Iran's nuclear threat and stand boldly with Israel,
> the only democracy in the Middle East . . . Think of our potential
> future together: 50 million evangelicals joining in common cause
> with 5 million Jewish people in America on behalf of Israel is a match
> made in heaven.[2]

The Pew Research Center recently discovered that 60% of evangelicals said they supported the State of Israel,[3] and 32% cited their religious beliefs as the primary reason for such support.[4]

The Unity Coalition for Israel, which brings together over 200 different autonomous organizations, is the largest pro-Israel network in the world. They claim to have 40 million active members, and lobby on behalf of Israel through 1,700 religious radio stations, 245 Christian TV stations, and 120 Christian newspapers.[5] Besides Christians United for Israel, the other three largest Christian Zionist organizations are the International Christian Embassy Jerusalem, Christian Friends of Israel, and Bridges for Peace. A powerful lobby movement? You bet. Christian Zionism is undoubtedly a dominant force shaping US foreign policy in the Middle East.[6] Why else will you not find a single serving US politician openly critical of Israel?

What about your presuppositions?

Discovering what the Bible has to say about the relationship between Israel and the church, in history and prophecy, is not just an academic exercise. What we believe and understand affects how we behave and act. Let me illustrate. If you believe the Bible predicts an imminent war of Armageddon, with Israel and the United States on one side and the Islamic and communist world on the other, then you will not lose any sleep over the stalled peace process. And when you read about yet more bloodshed and suffering in the Middle East, it will confirm what you already think is going to happen.

However, if you believe peace and reconciliation between Jews and Arabs in the Middle East is not only possible, but is also God's will; that the UN Declaration of Human Rights, while generally considered to be a humanist document, reflects Judeo-Christian principles; and that the consistent implementation of international law should form the basis for our diplomacy in the Middle East, then you will act to achieve peace with justice. Our presuppositions shape not only our beliefs but also our actions.

Postponement or fulfilment?

Why does this subject arouse such strong emotions among Christians, and evangelicals? Because the very gospel is at stake. The question to have at the back of your mind as you read further is this: Did the coming of Jesus, his death and resurrection and the founding of the church, fulfil or postpone the biblical prophecies concerning Israel? Is the church central to God's purposes on earth, or a temporary sideshow? In answering these questions, evangelicals tend to fall into one of two camps: covenantalists and dispensationalists. There are variations of each, but if you haven't heard of the terms before, you are not alone. Most evangelicals don't necessarily know which they are.

Covenantalism or dispensationalism?

Covenantalists tend to see the coming of Jesus as the fulfilment of the promises made to Israel, while dispensationalists tend to see it as the postponement of those promises. Covenantalists believe the Bible teaches that God has one 'chosen people' called out from among the nations. Dispensationalists believe the Bible teaches that God has two separate and distinct peoples – the church and Israel. They believe that the biblical promises made to the ancient Israelites apply to their Jewish descendants today. If covenantalists emphasize the continuity within God's progressive revelation, dispensationalists emphasize the discontinuity, distinguishing seven 'dispensations' in biblical history when God has tested humankind in a different way, and each time they have failed. They believe the present 'church age' or 'dispensation of grace' will also fail and soon come to an end. Then during the millennium, Jesus will reign as King of the Jews in Jerusalem, and the unfulfilled promises of the Old Testament will be realized.

Covenantalists tend to regard promises relating to the land, Jerusalem and the temple as annulled or fulfilled in the church. Dispensationalists usually see them as still in force and either being, or about to be, fulfilled in Israel today. Covenantalists are inclined to be neutral or positive about the future before the return of Jesus, being either amillennial or postmillennial. Dispensationalists are likely to be premillennial and pessimistic about the future.[7]

Table 1.1 compares and contrasts a dispensational and covenantal framework. There are many variations of each, and while there may appear to be a superficial similarity between them, remember that a covenantal framework emphasizes the continuity in God's sovereign purposes, whereas a dispensational one emphasizes discontinuity. The example of a covenantal framework is taken from Vaughan Roberts,[8] while the dispensational ages are taken from Cyrus Scofield.[9]

I'll come clean. I hold to a covenantal position. Does that mean I am biased? Yes. Let's be honest. We are all biased. The question is whether we realize it and have good reasons for our particular bias. In this book I have tried to be fair and accurate in describing positions

Biblical period	Covenantal description	Dispensational ages
Creation (Genesis 1 – 2)	The pattern of the kingdom	1. Innocency (Genesis 1:28)
Fall (Genesis 3 – 11)	The perished kingdom	2. Conscience (Genesis 3:23) 3. Human government (Genesis 8:20)
Abraham – Moses (Genesis 12 – Deuteronomy)	The promised kingdom	4. Promise (Genesis 12:1)
Israelites (Joshua – 2 Chronicles)	The partial kingdom	5. Law (Exodus 19:8)
Remnant (Ezra – Malachi)	The prophesied kingdom	
Jesus (Matthew – John)	The present kingdom	
Church (Acts – Revelation)	The proclaimed kingdom	6. Grace (John 1:17)
Heaven	The perfected kingdom	7. Kingdom (Ephesians 1:10)

Table 1.1.

with which I disagree. You can decide whether I have succeeded or failed. I believe the dispensational framework has been artificially imposed on the Scriptures, creating divisions that are not there and ignoring those that are there. The most obvious is Mark 1:1, 'The beginning of the good news about Jesus the Messiah'. While this momentous event doesn't warrant a new dispensation in Scofield's scheme, it does in mine!

Why is this such a controversial subject?

I have been called a lot of things over the years. The more printable ones include a liberal, an anti-Semite, and a supersessionist (an advocate of replacement theology). Let's begin by debunking these three red herrings.

Liberals and evangelicals

Dispensationalists like to think that they alone read the Bible literally and are more consistent than other Christians, who, for example, 'spiritualize' away the promises made to the Israelites. That is probably why they get upset when some conservative evangelicals beg to differ. It would be more accurate to say that sometimes dispensationalists accept a literal interpretation without acknowledging how Scripture interprets Scripture: for example, how Jesus and the apostles use Old Testament promises and terminology in new ways. By imposing seven 'dispensations' on the Bible, some dispensationalists seem to turn what is intended to be a unified plan of salvation for a sick world into separate isolation wards for different races.

Zionism and anti-Semitism

It is true that at various times in the past, churches and church leaders have tolerated or incited anti-Semitism and even attacks on Jewish people. Racism is a sin and without excuse. Anti-Semitism must be repudiated unequivocally. However, we must not confuse apples and oranges. Anti-Zionism is not the same thing as anti-Semitism, despite attempts to broaden the definition. Criticizing a political system as racist is not racist. Judaism is a religious system. Israel is a sovereign nation. Zionism is a political system. These three are not synonymous. I respect Judaism, repudiate anti-Semitism, encourage interfaith dialogue and defend Israel's right to exist within borders recognized by the international community and agreed with her neighbours. But like many Jews, I disagree with a political system that gives preference to expatriate Jews born elsewhere in the world, while denying the same rights to the Arab Palestinians born in the country itself. Jimmy Carter is not alone in describing the Zionism practised by the present government of Israel as a form of apartheid.[10]

Supersessionism or replacement theology

This is a favourite 'straw man' of Christian Zionists. They criticize their opponents for implying the church has 'replaced' Israel. The implication is that the Jewish people cease to have any role within the purposes of God. This is clearly refuted in Romans 9 – 11. However, the Scriptures are unambiguous in distinguishing between the old and new covenants. In Hebrews, the writer says, 'By calling this covenant "new", he has made the first one obsolete; and what is obsolete and outdated will soon disappear' (Hebrews 8:13). There is therefore, from a Christian perspective, no sense in which the old covenant can be viewed as still in force or applicable. On the night that Jesus was betrayed, after the supper he took the cup, saying, 'This cup is the new covenant in my blood, which is poured out for you' (Luke 22:20). When Jesus died on the cross, a new covenant was established with his precious blood that supersedes the basis of the old covenant. The writer to the Hebrews continues, 'For this reason Christ is the mediator of a new covenant, that those who are called may receive the promised eternal inheritance – now that he has died as a ransom to set them free from the sins committed under the first covenant' (Hebrews 9:15).

Here then is the biblical basis for a kind of supersessionism. But notice the succession is first of all from one covenant to another, not from Israel to the church. This is because both covenants were, in the first instance, made with the people of God who at that stage were predominantly Jewish. '"The days are coming," declares the LORD, "when I will make a new covenant with the house of Israel and with the house of Judah"' (Jeremiah 31:31). This is why Jesus initially sent his apostles only to the Jews. 'These twelve Jesus sent out with the following instructions: "Do not go among the Gentiles or enter any town of the Samaritans. Go rather to the lost sheep of Israel"' (Matthew 10:5–6). But when the majority rejected his ministry, Jesus warned, 'Therefore I tell you that the kingdom of God will be taken away from you and given to a people who will produce its fruit' (Matthew 21:43). Jesus here describes the succession that would occur within a generation. The apostle Peter, preaching after Pentecost and citing Moses, similarly warned those who rejected Jesus, 'Anyone who does not listen to him will be completely cut off from their people' (Acts 3:23). Covenantalists believe there has only ever been one people of God – whether under the old or new covenant – and one way to God – by grace alone and through faith alone. Both Israel and the church have been a mixed company of believers and unbelievers, Jews and Gentiles. Only God knows who is numbered among his faithful remnant. At various times in history it has been clearer than in others – for example, when all but the family of Noah perished, or when the entire generation who entered Sinai perished there, apart from a handful. That is why many covenantalists are uncomfortable describing the church as the 'new Israel'. The term never appears in the Bible. However, as we shall see in more detail in chapter 3, Peter uses language describing Israel and applies it to the church.

> They stumble because they disobey the message – which is also what they were destined for. But you are a chosen people, a royal priesthood, a holy nation, God's special possession, that you may declare the praises of him who called you out of darkness into his wonderful light. Once you were not a people, but now you are the people of God; once you had not received mercy, but now you have received mercy.
> (1 Peter 2:8–10)

It is not that the church has replaced Israel. Rather, in the new covenant church, God has fulfilled the promises originally made to the old covenant church. So, for example, when Jesus affirms Peter's declaration of faith and says, 'on this rock I will build my church, and the gates of death will not overcome it' (Matthew 16:18), the Greek word translated by 'church' is *ekklēsia* – the very word used in the Greek translation of the Old Testament to describe God's people.

Covenantalists are not liberal, anti-Semitic or into 'replacement' theology. That some dispensationalists believe Israel will 'replace' the church is another matter, but that can wait until chapter 3.

What is the relationship between religion and politics?

To get a handle on Christian Zionist theology, and the structure of this book, let me quote from two Jewish Rabbis. They both use an analogy that helps to illustrate the Zionist agenda. First, listen to Rabbi Shlomo Aviner: 'We should not forget ... that the supreme purpose of the ingathering of exiles and the establishment of our State is the building of the Temple. The Temple is at the very top of the

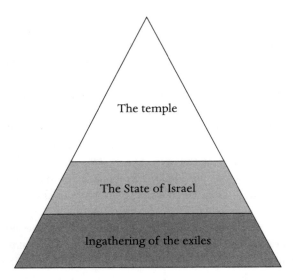

Figure 1.1.

pyramid'[11] (see Figure 1.1). This shows the relationship between religion and politics in modern Zionism. His vision is a kind of theocracy, which many Christian Zionists believe will occur when Jesus returns to reign as king of Israel in Jerusalem.

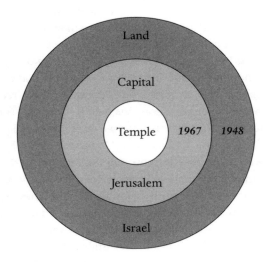

Figure 1.2.

Another Jewish rabbi, Yisrael Meida, uses a different analogy to make the same point: 'It is all a matter of sovereignty. He who controls the Temple Mount, controls Jerusalem. And he who controls Jerusalem, controls the land of Israel.'[12]

Imagine these three to be like three concentric rings of a target (see Figure 1.2). The land represents the outer ring, Jerusalem the middle ring and the temple is the centre ring. The three rings comprise the Zionist agenda by which the land was conquered in 1948, the Old City of Jerusalem was occupied in 1967, and the temple site, or Haram Al Sharif, is hotly contested between Zionists and Muslims. For the religious Zionist, Jewish or Christian, sovereignty over all three – land, city and temple – is essential and inextricably linked.

Is there an elephant in the room?

I hope you are beginning to see why this is such an important subject. There is a giant elephant in the room and it's time we started talking about it. As I intimated in the foreword, fear of being accused of anti-Semitism for challenging the Zionist agenda is enough to keep many evangelicals under their beds. In my view, and that of an increasing number of other evangelicals, it is time to speak out because Christian Zionism has become a formidable and dangerous movement. By portraying the modern state of Israel as God's chosen people on earth, the role of the church has been reduced in the eyes of many to providing moral and biblical justification for Israel's colonization of Palestine. Those who oppose her are demonized. While not all Christian Zionists endorse the apocalyptic views of Hal Lindsey and Tim LaHaye, the movement as a whole is nevertheless leading the West, and the church with it, into a confrontation with Islam. Using biblical terminology to justify a pre-emptive global war against the 'axis of evil' merely reinforces stereotypes, fuels extremism, incites fundamentalism and increases the likelihood of nuclear war. Do I think the Bible predicts all this? No I don't. In the next few chapters I will explain why.

It is not an understatement to say that what is at stake is our understanding of the gospel, the centrality of the cross, the role of the church and the nature of our missionary mandate, not least, to the beloved Jewish people.

So let's start with the source of our authority – the Bible, and how we should read it.

2. The Bible tells them so: Is it possible to read the Bible too literally?

You study the Scriptures diligently because you think that in them you possess eternal life. These are the very Scriptures that testify about me.

(John 5:39)

How do you read the Bible? With any literature we read, we bring certain presuppositions and expectations.[1] Presuppositions are important and we all have them. But knowing what they are is just as important, because they influence how we interpret what we read. If we don't know what they are, we are not aware of how they colour what we read. In this chapter we will consider three key presuppositions: it is important that we read the Bible literally, contextually and progressively. In particular, prophetic and apocalyptic Scripture needs special handling, and so we will examine this genre separately. We will then consider some of the pitfalls created when these biblical presuppositions are ignored, and illustrate how ultra-literalism leads to some very strange, tragic, and sometimes silly, interpretations. In conclusion, we will see how the Bible itself answers these forms of ultra-literalism.

Three important presuppositions when reading the Bible

1. We must read the Bible literally
To interpret the Bible literally is to interpret it *as literature* of various kinds – that is, according to the usual rules of grammar, speech, syntax, context and genre.

One of the distinctive hallmarks of evangelicals is the way in which we seek a literal, as opposed to an allegorical interpretation of biblical passages. We believe that God has revealed his purposes fully and finally in and through the Scriptures. That is why we call it 'revelation'. According to the book of Hebrews, 'For the word of God is alive and active. Sharper than any double-edged sword, it penetrates even to dividing soul and spirit, joints and marrow; it judges the thoughts and attitudes of the heart' (Hebrews 4:12). When I read the Bible, I make certain assumptions based on what it claims, as well as on my previous experiences – that it is indeed 'alive and active', the inspired Word of God; that the writers are trustworthy and telling the truth; and that God will reveal more of his perfect will for me as I submit my life to him and as I seek diligently to understand and apply his Word.

One important thing to remember – we must never apply a passage to ourselves before we have understood its original purpose. It may be tempting to imagine a passage was written just for me, but it wasn't. The Bible was not written to me. Let me say that again – the Bible was not written to me – it was written *for* me. There is a big difference. When I read a passage in the Bible I must remember I am reading it over the shoulder of the person or group of people who it was originally written to. This is why it is essential that we read a passage within its historical and cultural context.

At the same time we must not forget that God wants to reveal himself to us through the Bible. God is not hiding from us or playing a game in the Bible. Evangelicals hold to the idea of scriptural perspicuity – that God's purposes are clear and unambiguous. The Bible is, as Alec Motyer says, 'like a good detective story: clues come first; solutions follow'.[2] It is not, however, like a jigsaw puzzle, with some of the pieces missing. This is why we should not search for 'Bible codes' or hidden messages.

The goal of interpretation is to understand the meaning of the text that the biblical writers intended to communicate. In the divine–

human concurrent activity of inspiration, God intended to communicate with his people, so biblical texts convey meaning at both the divine and human levels. An inspired and authoritative Bible has significance and relevance beyond its original circumstances, and there may be many applications. We need to work hard at interpretation. Thankfully, godly people have dedicated their lives to studying God's Word carefully in the original Hebrew, Aramaic and Greek, and have written some really useful commentaries to help us.[3] So we must read the Bible literally.

2. We must read the Bible contextually

Someone, probably famous, once said, 'A text without a context is a pretext for a proof text.' Clearly, understanding the context and purpose of a passage is important in order to find its meaning. This includes the historical, cultural and theological contexts. It is also important to ascertain what kind of writing it is – prose, poetry, parable or prophecy. Here are some important questions to ask of a passage:

- Who was the writer?
- To whom is it being written?
- What kind of literature is it?
- What is the cultural and historical context?
- What is the meaning of the text (our only access to the author's intention)?
- How was the text interpreted by those who first received it?
- Why was the author saying/writing it?

How we answer these questions will clearly influence both our interpretation and application. It is therefore important to try to answer these questions before seeking to make specific application to ourselves and especially to events happening today.[4]

So is it possible to read the Bible in an ultra-literalist way? Yes, especially when people try to apply Old Testament terms like 'chosen' and 'inheritance' today, without first reading them in their original context or in light of the New Testament, which gives them new meaning. This error also occurs when it is claimed that contemporary events were prophesied in the Bible – such as the rise of the European

Community or Saddam Hussein's régime. This kind of speculative prophetic reading of the Bible became popular in the nineteenth century through the influence of John Nelson Darby, who helped found the Brethren churches, and among the Adventist and millennial sects. One of Darby's followers in America, Cyrus Scofield, popularized this kind of interpretation through his *Scofield Reference Bible*, which became the most popular study Bible in the first half of the twentieth century.

> Not one instance exists of a 'spiritual' or figurative fulfilment of prophecy. Jerusalem is always Jerusalem, Israel is always Israel, Zion is always Zion ... Prophecies may never be spiritualised, but are always literal.[5]

The problem with this kind of wooden literalism is that it leads to rather bizarre and sometimes inconsistent interpretations. For example, fans of Israel like to emphasize passages in which words such as 'eternal', 'everlasting' or 'forever' are used in connection with the giving of the land, Jerusalem or the temple to the Jewish people.

Sometimes the immediate context of a passage indicates that a 'forever' isn't always to be taken literally. In Isaiah 32, for example, God warns that Jerusalem 'will become a wasteland for ever' (32:14), but in the following verse he adds, 'till the Spirit is poured on us...' (32:15). Similarly, words such as 'everlasting' are sometimes used for emphasis rather than necessarily to indicate something eternal. In Genesis 17:13, for example, circumcision is described as an 'everlasting covenant', while in Psalm 74:3, the destroyed temple is described as 'everlasting ruins'. In many cases, the context indicates that 'a very long time' is intended. Sometimes similar words are used to emphasize the seriousness of God's judgment. Here is one example:

> But if you do not obey me to keep the Sabbath day holy by not carrying any load as you come through the gates of Jerusalem on the Sabbath day, then I will kindle an unquenchable fire in the gates of Jerusalem that will consume her fortresses.
> (Jeremiah 17:27)

Sometimes, a 'wooden' literalism will conflict with history or contradict another passage in the Bible. Table 2.1 shows some examples.

Old Testament promise	New Testament fulfilment
I have consecrated this temple, which you have built, by putting my Name there for ever. My eyes and my heart will always be there. (1 Kings 9:3)	I did not see a temple in the city, because the Lord God Almighty and the Lamb are its temple. (Revelation 21:22)
No-one but the Levites may carry the ark of God, because the LORD chose them to carry the ark of the LORD and to minister before him for ever ... Aaron was set apart, he and his descendants for ever, to consecrate the most holy things, to offer sacrifices before the LORD, to minister before him and to pronounce blessings in his name for ever. (1 Chronicles 15:2; 23:13)	If perfection could have been attained through the Levitical priesthood ... why was there still need for another priest to come, one in the order of Melchizedek, not in the order of Aaron? For when the priesthood is changed, the law must be changed also. (Hebrews 7:11–12)
Once for all, I have sworn by my holiness – and I will not lie to David – that his line will continue for ever and his throne endure before me like the sun. (Psalm 89:35–36)	Jesus said, 'My kingdom is not of this world. If it were, my servants would fight to prevent my arrest by the Jewish leaders. But now my kingdom is from another place.' (John 18:36)

Table 2.1.

The New Testament shows that Jesus himself was often misunderstood by those who interpreted his figurative language in a wooden, literal sense. John's Gospel contains several instances. For example, after he had cleansed the temple and was asked by the Pharisees for a sign, Jesus replied, 'Destroy this temple and I will raise it again in three days' (John 2:19). They thought he meant their temple, and Jesus did not bother to correct their error. In the next few chapters, Nicodemus wonders how he can enter his mother's womb again (John 3:4); the Samaritan woman believes Jesus is offering her free water on tap (4:15); and the religious leaders fear Jesus is advocating cannibalism by saying they must eat his body and drink his blood (6:51–52). So one of the most common mistakes made by people who heard Jesus first-hand was to take his words too literally. It is ironic that people still make the same mistake today.

3. We must read the Bible progressively

Here is another biblical presupposition we can observe in these verses from Paul's second letter to Timothy: 'All Scripture is God-breathed and is useful for teaching, rebuking, correcting and training in righteousness, so that all God's people may be thoroughly equipped for every good work' (2 Timothy 3:16–17).

The Bible is the very Word of God. And remember that when Paul was inspired to write that sentence, he would probably have had the Hebrew Scriptures in mind. We must therefore place a particular book or passage within the progressive revelation of God's will. Being rooted in history, God's revelation is progressive in the sense that he reveals more of his purposes as time goes on. And remember that the Bible as history is a 'one-way street'. We therefore usually interpret earlier passages in the light of later ones. So, for example, the writer to the Hebrews says 'The law is only a shadow of the good things that are coming – not the realities themselves' (Hebrews 10:1). Paul amplifies this in Galatians:

> Before the coming of this faith, we were held in custody under the law, locked up until the faith that was to come would be revealed. So the law was put in charge of us until Christ came that we might be justified by faith. Now that this faith has come, we are no longer under the supervision of the law.
> (Galatians 3:23–25)

The word translated by 'put in charge' was used by the Greeks to describe the role of a household slave or servant, who was in some way responsible for a child's care and upbringing (see also 1 Corinthians 4:15).

So, if in the words of Paul, 'the law' does not 'lead us to Christ', as intended, then our interpretation of it is likely to be defective. What is the relationship between the Old and New Testaments? Alec Motyer helpfully summarizes five aspects of the relationship – confirmation, finalization, dependence, reaffirmation and completion:

The five are as follows: *confirmation, i.e.* the unfolding of truth in the Bible, and especially in the narrative words and deeds of Jesus, confirm earlier lines of revelation; *finalization, i.e.* where the earlier revelation has embedded the truth in provisional forms, guarded it with temporary safeguards, or couched it in contemporary but ultimately inadequate thought-forms, it is then stated in its final form; *dependence, i.e.* the final statement of a truth assumes all that has gone before and cannot be understood without reference to the earlier words or events; *reaffirmation, i.e.* some items in the Old Testament seem at first sight to be out of step with the character of Jesus and the revelation vouchsafed in him, yet the New Testament does not reject but affirms them; *completion, i.e.* the Bible expresses a progressive revelation, an accumulating body of truth in which the New Testament rounds out the Old.[6]

Since God is the author and inspiration of all the Scriptures, what he says in one passage will not contradict what he says in another. We must be careful therefore not to create tension that does not exist, especially between the Old and New Testaments, but instead to look for the flow of revelation (see Figure 2.1), just as Jesus instructed the Pharisees. 'You study the Scriptures diligently because you think that in them you possess eternal life. These are the very Scriptures that testify about me' (John 5:39). If we have come to know Jesus as our

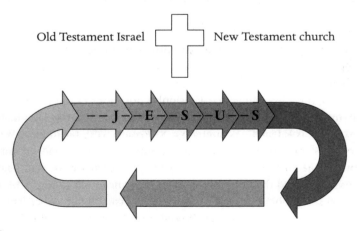

Figure 2.1.

personal Lord and Saviour, we will read the Hebrew Scriptures with Christian eyes – the way Jesus and his apostles did.

Even the apostles didn't always do this straightaway. They brought their Jewish presuppositions with them, which sometimes coloured their hopes and expectations. For example, after Christ's resurrection and just before his ascension to heaven, the apostles were still confused about whether he was going to restore the kingdom to the Jewish people and defeat the Romans (see Acts 1:6–7). On a previous occasion, on the road to Emmaus, Jesus had gently rebuked some of them. 'How foolish you are, and how slow of heart to believe all the prophets have spoken! ... And beginning with Moses and all the Prophets, he explained to them what was said in all the Scriptures concerning himself' (Luke 24:27).

After Pentecost, the Holy Spirit helped the apostles to see that Jesus was the Saviour of all nations and not just King of the Jews, and that his kingly rule extended over the whole world and was not just limited to Israel. The Acts of the Apostles and the epistles show how they came to recognize how Jesus was the fulfilment of the hope and expectation of the Hebrew Scriptures.

We too need the same illuminating work of the Holy Spirit as we read the Bible, to see the harmony and progression in God's purposes. D. L. Moody often used to say 'The Bible without the Holy Spirit is a sundial by moonlight.' It is certainly dull and you are bound to get a wrong reading. We must take care to read the Bible literally, contextually and progressively.

Interpreting prophetic and apocalyptic Scriptures

As the new millennium approached, there was a marked rise in the number of books published on Bible prophecy. One commentator called it PMT – Pre-Millennial Tension! A notorious example, perhaps not surprisingly now out of print, but easily found in second-hand bookstores, is Edgar C. Whisenant's, *88 Reasons Why the Rapture Will Be in 1988*.[7] On 1 January 1989, he published a vain second attempt entitled, *The Final Shout: Rapture Report 1989*.[8] I suspect he had been writing it toward the end of 1988 as an insurance policy. Edgar, bless him, is sadly not alone. If you want to read about other failed prophets, check out *Doomsday Delusions* by Marvin Pate and Calvin Haines.[9]

Prophecy	Apocalyptic
Initially spoken then later written	Initially written
Separate brief message	Longer and more repetitive
Plain language	Symbolic language (e.g. animals) Dualism is common (Jesus and angels vs Satan and the Anti-Christ)
Castigates nominal believers	Confirms and encourages remnant
Focus on repentance and faith	Pessimistic about human ability to change events

Table 2.2.

There are some ways in which prophecy differs from other apocalyptic literature[10] (see Table 2.2). Prophecy is associated with forth-telling and foretelling God's Word. Invariably the prophets had a message for their contemporaries (forth-telling) and a message concerning the distant future (foretelling). Sometimes it is difficult to distinguish one from the other, as in Isaiah 7:1–17. Apocalyptic literature, which means 'revelation' or 'unveiling', tends to focus only on the events leading to the end of time.

Both prophecy and apocalyptic literature share much in common. They both emphasize God's sovereignty in human affairs as well as his future intervention at the end of time to deal with sin and bring justice and peace. Both promise that the faithful who stand firm will be redeemed. The writings of the prophets are clearly identified in the Bible and include the writings of sixteen prophets from Isaiah to Malachi, together with others such as Samuel, Elijah, Elisha and even Saul (1 Samuel 10:5–11). The biblical passages associated with the apocalyptic include Ezekiel 38 – 39; Daniel 7 – 12; Matthew 24; Mark 13; Luke 21; 2 Thessalonians 2; and Revelation 6 – 19.

Sometimes biblical books contain both the prophetic and the apocalyptic. The book of Revelation is one example (see Table 2.3).

Prophetic	Apocalyptic
Revelation 1 – 3. A series of exhortations to the churches of the first century.	Revelation 4 – 22. A series of heavenly visions about the future.

Table 2.3.

It is important when reading apocalyptic literature to know a little bit more about its common characteristics before attempting to interpret and apply it. Marvin Pate and Calvin Haines helpfully list the typical characteristics of apocalyptic material. These include:

- The writer often goes on a journey with a celestial guide who shows him interesting sites and comments on them.
- The information is usually communicated through visions.
- Visions often contain strange or even enigmatic symbolism including depictions of animals and other living beings.
- Visions are usually pessimistic about people being able to change the outcome.
- Visions usually end with God destroying evil through his personal and cataclysmic intervention.
- The vision is intended to comfort and sustain the righteous remnant who will be rewarded when God establishes his kingdom.[11]

Historically, biblical apocalyptic literature arose between the time of the Babylonian captivity (Ezekiel and Daniel), through the return of the exiles (Zechariah), to the Greek and then Roman occupation of Palestine (Revelation). Therefore, the time between around 586 BC and AD 100 was one of great ferment and anxiety for the Jewish people. The apocalyptic writings describe the rise and fall of empires as well as rulers who at various times tolerated or persecuted God's people. Sometimes the text itself helps us to understand that what is described, while using human imagery, is intended to be interpreted figuratively or symbolically. So, for example, in Zechariah's vision of the future, we meet Joshua the High Priest 'standing before the angel of the LORD and Satan' (Zechariah 3:1). Just when you want to know more about this enigmatic person – remember Joshua is Hebrew for Jesus – Zechariah drops a hint: 'Listen, High Priest Joshua, you and your associates seated before you, you who are symbolic of things to come: I am going to bring my servant, the Branch' (Zechariah 3:8). So Joshua and his friends, whether a literal person or not, signify or symbolize future events, just as the term 'Branch' is understood as a Messianic title for Jesus (see Isaiah 4:2; Jeremiah 23:5).

This is a good illustration of how, at the same time, apocalyptic literature portrays 'history' between the now and the not yet – between the present and God's future intervention to rescue and vindicate his people. This is the period known as the 'end times' or 'last days'. We must recognize, however, that these terms have been used for rather a long while, and don't refer just to events since 1948 or 1967. Quoting Isaiah 44:3, for example, Peter describes the events of the Day of Pentecost as the fulfilment of these last days (Acts 2:16–17; see also Hebrews 1:2). We must not therefore be naïve in thinking we alone are living in the end times. Let me quote once more from Pate and Haines:

> Put another way, end-time prophecy, because it more often than not emerged from a persecuted minority, is a coded language in need of deciphering. The reason for the use of coded language is obvious – it protected both author and recipients from the dominant, oppressing regimes of the day. Hence, for example, the prevalence of heavenly visions, enigmatic symbolism (for example, beasts representing political empires), gematria (figurative meaning attached to numbers such as 666), dualism (the clash of people groups described in terms of a struggle between supernatural powers). As such, eschatological prophecy's primary focus concerned the particular life setting of the biblical author and recipients, though its parameters also include the distant future.[12]

While apocalyptic literature is like an animated picture book, full of detail, movement and action, it is not a puzzle book intended to confuse. That is why it is important to focus on the broad themes and not get hung up on the detail. Michael Wilcock makes this very helpful assessment:

The conviction that the Revelation really is meant to reveal truth, and not to obscure it, and that its treasures really do lie on the surface if one looks for them in the right light, is by no means the same as a belief that its meaning will be spelt out for us verbally, with logic and precision ... It is no use reading Revelation as though it were a Paul-type theological treatise in a slightly different idiom, or a Luke-style history projected into the future.[13]

This is why apocalyptic literature like Revelation should be interpreted in harmony with the teachings of the entire Bible. There are, for example, over 400 references or allusions to the Old Testament in the book of Revelation. William Hendriksen reminds us that 'In emphasizing this basis of the Apocalyptic visions in the subsoil of the sacred Scriptures we must always bear in mind that it is wise to proceed from the clearer to the more obscure and never vice versa.'[14]

To sum up, there are two basic errors that ultra-literalists make regarding prophetic and apocalyptic literature. First, they ignore the historical setting of the passages and the way in which prophecies have already been fulfilled. Second, they read back into the passages contemporary events and develop novel ways to interpret them, as if they were speaking of present-day readers. This heresy is not new. It's good to remember the words of Martin Luther who said of the book of Revelation, 'everyone thinks of the book what ever his spirit imparts'.[15] Let's look at some examples to illustrate this:

Five common mistakes made by ultra-literalists
Here are some more common mistakes made by ultra-literalists when biblical presuppositions are ignored:

1. Transient literalism
When Christian writers interpret contemporary events in the light of prophecy, they run into difficulties. For example, Hal Lindsey insisted that Russia's place in history was predicted in the Bible (see Table 2.4).

As Russia declined, Lindsey switched his emphasis to Islamic fundamentalism. While *The Late Great Planet Earth* (1970) suggested that we were threatened by 'The Russian force',[16] in the *Oracle Commentaries* (2006), that had morphed into a 'Russian-Syrian-Iranian Axis'.[17]

1980's *Countdown to Armageddon*	*Planet Earth* 2000 A D
Today, the Soviets are without question the strongest power on the face of the earth. Let's look at recent history to see how the Russians rose to the might predicted for them thousands of years ago.[18]	We see Russia as no longer a world threat, but a regional power with a world-class military – exactly what Ezekiel 38 and 39 predicted it would be.[19]

Table 2.4.

Another favourite theme of prophecy pundits is 'Babylon the Great' (Revelation 14:8; 17:5), variously interpreted as the Roman Empire, the Vatican, and the European Community. If we take the Bible literally, surely 'Babylon' is Babylon?

Charles Dyer's *The Rise of Babylon: Sign of the End Times*[20] indeed suggested that Babylon would be rebuilt before the final battle of Armageddon, and then he showed how Saddam Hussein was apparently rebuilding it. The cover shows Saddam in uniform, in front of a statue of Nebuchadnezzar. With Saddam's untimely demise, events in Iraq do not appear to be heading in the predicted direction. In 2004, Dyer's sequel[21] presents a toppled Saddam alongside an image of the new enemy – Osama Bin Laden. The actors may change, but the same confident assurance of 'Bible prophecy coming true' remains.

2. Speculative literalism

Hal Lindsey adopts a similar approach to apocalyptic descriptions. Since someone in the first century could not understand scientific developments in the twentieth, the apostle John was forced to 'illustrate them with phenomena of the first century; for instance, a thermonuclear war looked to him like a giant volcanic eruption spewing fire and brimstone'. The symbolism in Revelation is the result of 'a first-Century man being catapulted in God's time machine up to the end of the twentieth century',[22] and returning to describe what he saw.

Capitalizing on the *Bible Code* craze, Lindsey's *Apocalypse Code* takes John's 'locusts' for helicopters; 'horses prepared for battle' as heavily armed attack helicopters; 'crowns of gold' for helmets and so on.[23] The superficial appeal of this kind of interpretation is short-lived, as the wreckage of previous false claims testifies.

3. Contradictory literalism

While ultra-literalists claim to provide 'consistent interpretation', they nonetheless reach very different conclusions. See for instance how M. R. DeHann and Hal Lindsey contradict one another (see Table 2.5).

M. R. DeHann (1946)	Hal Lindsey (1973)
In Revelation 9:13–21 we have a description of an army of two hundred million horsemen ... seems to be a supernatural army of horrible beings, probably demons, who are permitted to plague the unrepentant sinners on the earth.[24]	The four angels of Revelation 9:14–15 will mobilize an army of 200 million soldiers from east of the Euphrates ... I believe these 200 million troops are Red Chinese soldiers accompanied by other Eastern allies.[25]

Table 2.5.

While for DeHann the 200 million are 'demonic horsemen',[26] for Lindsey they are 'Chinese soldiers',[27] and indeed their horses may be mobilized ballistic missile launchers![28] These writers cannot all be right – unless we are talking about 200 million demonically possessed Chinese soldiers on horseback.

In his 1940 commentary, regularly reprinted since then, William Hendriksen raised several important questions about this kind of interpretation:

> Do these symbols refer to specific events, single happenings, dates or persons in history? For if they do, then we may well admit that we cannot interpret them. Because among the thousands of dates and events and persons in history that show certain traits of resemblance to the symbol in question, who is able to select the one and only date, event or person that was forecast by this particular symbol?[29]

How can we tell which interpretation is correct if we don't first allow Scripture to interpret Scripture within its historical context?

4. Enhanced literalism

For ultra-literalists, sometimes the biblical text seems to need a little 'enhancing' to make their interpretation more obvious. When Hal Lindsey interprets a biblical text, he often adds words [in brackets] purportedly to guide us. Here are just a couple of examples. 'Therefore when you see the Abomination which was spoken of through Daniel the prophet, standing in the holy place [of the rebuilt Temple] (let the reader understand), then let those who are in Judea flee to the mountains.'[30] Here the prophecy is assumed to refer to a supposedly rebuilt temple, rather than to the desecration of Herod's temple by the Romans and Zealots. His interpretation of Daniel 11:40–45 is similarly imaginative:

> At the time of the end the King of the South [the Muslim Confederacy] will engage him [the False Prophet of Israel] in battle, and the King of the North [Russia] will storm out against him with chariots and cavalry and a great fleet of ships. He [the Russian Commander] will invade many countries and sweep through them like a flood. He will also invade the Beautiful Land [Israel]. Many countries will fall, but Edom, Moab and the leaders of Ammon [Jordan] will be delivered from his hand.[31]

The perception of Russia as the end-times enemy of Israel is largely the product of Scofield's imaginative speculations. The passage which sparks most controversy is Ezekiel 38:15–16, in which Scofield takes 'Gog' and 'Magog' to refer to Russia. Notice also how Scofield enhances the text:

> That the primary reference is to the northern (European) powers, headed up by Russia, all agree . . . 'Gog' is the prince, 'Magog' his land. The reference to Meshech and Tubal (Moscow and Tobolsk) is a clear mark of identification.[32]

Ultra-literalists have perpetuated the principle of 'enhancing' the text to reinforce their own interpretations. The myth that Gog and Magog refer to Russia is repeated ad nauseam.[33] Tim LaHaye insists, 'Etymologically, the Gog and Magog of Ezekiel 38 and 39 can only mean modern-day Russia.'[34] The theory has nevertheless been discredited by biblical scholars and etymologists alike.[35] John B. Taylor offers this critical assessment. 'Interpretation needs to correspond to the contexts, and attempts to read too much into the incidentals of the prophecy betray the ingenuity of the speculator rather than the sobriety of the exegete.'[36]

5. Arbitrary literalism

Sooner or later, someone was bound to suggest that the United States of America appears in the Bible. Several authors have tried.[37] Lindsey appears to be one of the first. His reading of Revelation 12:14–17, 'The woman was given the two wings of a great eagle, so that she might fly to the place prepared for her in the desert' takes the passage to refer to 'some massive airlift' transporting escaping Jews from the Holocaust. 'Since the eagle is the national symbol of the United States, it's possible that the airlift will be made available by aircraft from the US Sixth Fleet in the Mediterranean.'[38] Lindsey does not explain why 'the eagle' should mean the United States, rather than Germany or the Czech Republic for instance. Nor does he explain why in Revelation it refers to modern aircraft, while in Exodus 19:4, Deuteronomy 32:11–12 and Isaiah 40:31 it does not. This is hardly evidence for a consistent 'literal interpretation'.

Mike Evans has caused an even bigger splash with his latest offering, *The American Prophecies*:

> Is America in prophecy? Yes, it is. As a Middle East analyst and minister who has worked closely with leaders in that region for decades, I tended to be sceptical of attempts to come up with schemes to plug America into prophetic interpretations. I have often referred to such teachers as 'Pop Prophecy Peddlers'. But, after thousands of hours of research, I am totally convinced that America is found in prophecy, and I believe you will, too, after reading [my] book.[39]

Even the reviewer for Amazon observes that actual quotes from Scripture are rather sparse.[40] Controversially, Evans goes on to claim

> September 11 would never have happened if America had fought the same bigotry in the 1990s rather than trying to appease it. Millions of

Jews would be living today if anti-Semitism had not been ignored in the 1920s and 1930s. The Great Depression, as well as other American tragedies, happened because of America's pride and challenge to God Almighty's plan.[41]

The danger with this kind of prophetic speculation is that it can become a self-fulfilling prophecy. This is how D. S. Russell summarizes the dilemma:

> One rather frightening by-product of this process of interpretation is that it is easy to create the very situation which is being described so that the interpretation given brings about its own fulfilment. Russia, for example, is to be destroyed by nuclear attack – and scripture must be fulfilled! It needs little imagination to understand the consequences of such a belief, especially if held with deep conviction by politicians and the military who have the power to press the button and to execute the judgment thus prophesied and foreordained.[42]

Answering the ultra-literalists

The fundamental error these ultra-literalists make is that they fail to recognize how Jesus and the apostles reinterpreted the Old Testament. Instead, texts are made to speak about present and future events almost as if the New Testament had never been written. The implicit assumption is that somehow Old and New Testaments at times run parallel into the future, the former speaking of Israel and the latter of the church, almost independent of one another (see Figure 2.2).

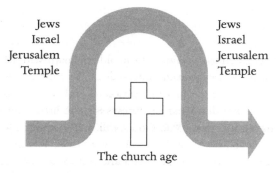

Figure 2.2. Old Testament promises await future fulfilment.

The problem with this kind of reasoning is that it actually contradicts the Bible. Jesus and the apostles tell us quite plainly that some parts of the Hebrew Scriptures have been fulfilled, annulled or superseded. In Mark 7, for example, the Pharisees challenged Jesus because his disciples didn't ceremonially wash their hands before eating. Jesus replied: ' "Don't you see that nothing that enters you from the outside can defile you? For it doesn't go into your heart but into your stomach, and then out of your body." (In saying this, Jesus declared all foods clean.)' (Mark 7:18–19).

In just one sentence, Jesus annulled the restrictive Levitical laws that determined what food could and could not be eaten. Bacon was now kosher. God has to give the apostle Peter a vision of unclean food and command him to eat it before he realizes that in Christ there is no distinction between Jew and Gentile (Acts 10:11–15). When Peter encounters Cornelius, a Gentile who has come to believe in Jesus, he finally gets it. 'I now realize how true it is that God does not show favouritism but accepts those from every nation who fear him and do what is right' (Acts 10:34–35).

Until then, Peter had thought that the Jewish people enjoyed an exclusive and special relationship with God denied to Gentiles. As we shall see in the next chapter, through the death of Jesus, 'the people of God' now embraces all peoples. The book of Hebrews explains the reasons for this:

> In the past God spoke to our ancestors through the prophets at many times and in various ways, but in these last days he has spoken to us by his Son, whom he appointed heir of all things, and through whom also he made the universe.
> (Hebrews 1:1–2)

The writer goes on to explain that the old covenant with Israel is now obsolete because it has been superseded. 'By calling this covenant "new", he has made the first one obsolete; and what is obsolete and outdated will soon disappear' (Hebrews 8:13). A little later the writer explains that Jesus came to do God's will. In so doing, 'He sets aside the first to establish the second' (Hebrews 10:9). His perfect atonement, made once for all, superseded and 'set aside' the need for any further animal sacrifices. This is because in the death of Jesus, God has 'cancelled the charge of our legal indebtedness' (Colossians 2:14), 'destroyed the barrier ... by setting aside in his flesh the law' (Ephesians 2:14–15). This is why it is fundamental that we read the Bible with Christian eyes, and that we interpret the old covenant in the light of the new covenant, not the other way round. The writer of Hebrews explains why the coming of Jesus, the Light of the World, made such a difference:

> The law is only a shadow of the good things that are coming – not the realities themselves. For this reason it can never, by the same sacrifices repeated endlessly year after year, make perfect those who draw near to worship.
> (Hebrews 10:1)

Paul draws out the implications of this for Christ's followers, both Jewish and Gentile. 'Therefore do not let anyone judge you by what you eat or drink, or with regard to a religious festival ... or a Sabbath day. These are a shadow of the things that were to come; the reality, however, is found in Christ' (Colossians. 2:16–17).

The question is therefore not whether the promises of the Old Testament should be understood literally or allegorically. It is instead a question of whether they should be understood in terms of old covenant 'shadow' or in terms of new covenant 'reality'. This is the basic error some Christians make when they apply Old Testament passages to the Jewish people and Israel today, without interpreting them in the light of what the New Testament has to say.

If the Hebrew Scriptures, just as much as the Christian Scriptures, are indeed primarily concerned with telling the story of God's rescue mission, in sending his incarnate Son, the Lord Jesus Christ, to be the Saviour of the world (Luke 24:27; John 5:39), then the primary question we need to ask of any passage is surely this: how does it relate to God's purposes fully and finally revealed in Jesus?

In the next chapter we will explore the biblical concept of 'chosenness' and ask the question: who exactly are God's 'chosen people'?

Chapter summary points

- We must interpret the Bible literally, contextually and progressively.
- We must see how the New Testament helps to interpret the Old Testament.
- We must take special care when interpreting prophecy and the apocalyptic Scriptures.
- We must avoid the temptation to allow contemporary events to determine our interpretation.
- The ultimate question of any passage is this: how does it relate to God's purposes fully and finally revealed in Jesus?

Passages to review
John 5:24–40; Colossians 2:8–19; 2 Timothy 3:10 – 4:5; Hebrews 1:1–14; 4:1–13; 10:1–25.

Questions for further study

1. What are my presuppositions as I read the Bible?
2. Which books or writers have influenced or shaped them?
3. How was the coming of Jesus the fulfilment or postponement of the promises made to Israel?
4. How is Jesus central to the Bible message?
5. In what ways is the Old Testament a 'shadow' of the New Testament?
6. Which aspects of the old covenant are now 'obsolete' for Christians?

3. Israel and the church: Who are God's chosen people?

How often have you heard the Jewish people described as God's 'chosen people'? Probably so often that you have never even questioned it. It is so ingrained that to deny it is often seen as evidence of anti-Semitism. As is the assumption that God blesses and curses nations on the basis of how they treat Israel – which is sometimes used as a threat. This view goes back to Genesis 12:3. Jerry Falwell, for example, says God is blessing America because 'America has been kind to the Jew'.[1] He claims that God 'will bless those who bless the Jews and curse whoever curses the Jews'.[2] That is why Christians United for Israel conducts 'A Night to Honor Israel'[3] in as many cities as possible, so that God will continue to bless America and Canada.

It may surprise you to discover that the New Testament never uses the term 'chosen' to describe the Jewish people. It is used only of those who follow Jesus. Does that mean God has two separate 'chosen people'? Some like to think so. They are usually called 'dispensationalists', and this is a popular viewpoint among evangelicals in the United States.

In this chapter we will begin by looking at the evidence for two 'chosen people' and then tackle the 'blessing and cursing' issue. Next we will examine the term 'Israel' in the Old and New Testaments, and we shall consider some of the biblical imagery God uses to describe his relationship to his people, such as the analogy of the vine and the vineyard. We also need to define what we mean by words like 'Jew', 'chosen' and 'children of God'.

The sand and the stars

John Nelson Darby, one of the founders of the Brethren movement, along with Cyrus Scofield, through his *Scofield Reference Bible*, popularized the novel idea that God has two separate plans – one being fulfilled through the church, the other through Israel. According to Scofield, 'Comparing then, what is said in Scripture concerning Israel and the Church, we find that in origin, calling, promise, worship, principles of conduct and future destiny all is contrast.'[4] Lewis Sperry Chafer, one of Scofield's students, elaborates on this alleged dichotomy between Israel and the church:

> The dispensationalist believes that throughout the ages God is pursuing two distinct purposes: one related to the earth with earthly people and earthly objectives involved which is Judaism; while the other is related to heaven with heavenly people and heavenly objectives involved, which is Christianity . . . Israel is an eternal nation, heir to an eternal land, with an eternal kingdom, on which David rules from an eternal throne, so that in eternity . . . never the twain, Israel and church, shall meet.[5]

If you imagine the way railway lines run parallel but never meet, that is how many dispensationalists believe Israel and the church remain separate.

This leads John Hagee, for example, to a novel interpretation of Genesis 22 (see Figure 3.1), where God promises Abraham, 'I will surely

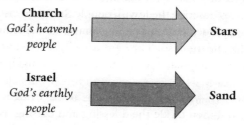

Figure 3.1. Genesis 22:17 according to John Hagee.

bless you and make your descendants as numerous as the stars in the sky and as the sand on the seashore' (Genesis 22:17). Hagee states,

> Stars are heavenly, not earthly. They represent the church, spiritual Israel. The 'sand of the shore' on the other hand, is earthly and represents an earthly kingdom with a literal Jerusalem as the capital city. Both stars and sand exist at the same time, and neither ever replaces the other. Just so, the nation of Israel and spiritual Israel, the church, exist at the same time and do not replace each other.[6]

However, Hagee's colourful interpretation doesn't quite fit with the way Scripture interprets Scripture. Around 430 BC Nehemiah thanked God that the promise made to Abraham had already been fulfilled: 'You made their children as numerous as the stars in the sky' (Nehemiah 9:23). Notice Nehemiah likens Jews, not Gentiles, to the stars in the sky. Maybe they are the sand not the stars . . .

Nevertheless, this view remains popular among many evangelicals and fundamentalists in the United States. It also lies behind best-sellers such as Hal Lindsey's The Late Great Planet Earth, as well as Tim LaHaye's blockbuster Left Behind series.

While not all Christian Zionists buy into dispensationalism and the distinction between Israel and the church, they nevertheless believe that the Jews remain God's 'chosen people', enjoying a unique relationship, status and purpose, separate from any promises made to the church. They typically also believe that the promises made to Abraham in Genesis are being fulfilled in and through the physical descendants of Isaac, Jacob and Joseph, who are living in Israel today. Based on passages like Genesis 15, Christian Friends of Israel, for example, state, 'The Bible teaches that Israel (people, land, nation) has a Divinely ordained and glorious future, and that God has neither rejected nor replaced his Jewish people.'[7] Similarly, Jews for Jesus distinguish between God's continuing purposes for Israel and those concerning the church.

> We believe that Israel exists as a covenant people through whom God continues to accomplish his purposes and that the Church is an elect people in accordance with the new covenant, comprising both Jews and Gentiles who acknowledge Jesus as Messiah and Redeemer.[8]

David Brickner affirms the novel position first propounded by J. N. Darby, that the Jews remain 'God's chosen people', while the church is merely 'a parenthesis' to God's future plans for the Jews.[9] These authors and organizations believe Jewish people somehow continue to enjoy a special covenant relationship with God apart from through Jesus Christ.

It is ironic that some Christian Zionists accuse their critics of holding to a 'replacement theology' – the idea that the church has replaced Israel – when many actually believe Israel will soon replace the church as God's people on earth. They have, as Dr Gilbert Bilezikian observed, made 'Israel the bride and the Church the concubine'.[10]

Blessing and cursing Israel

The belief that God judges people, organizations and nations on the basis of how they treat the Jewish people and the State of Israel is rooted in one of the promises God made to Abraham. 'I will bless those who bless you, and whoever curses you I will curse; and all peoples on earth will be blessed through you' (Genesis 12:3). The International Christian Embassy, Jerusalem (ICEJ) uses Genesis 12:3 to encourage Christians to pray for Israel and to support their work financially.

> This promise was given to the Hebrew Patriarchs Abraham and Jacob – or Israel. So whoever blesses Israel will be blessed. But how can you bless Israel? The answer is easy: prayer; finances; come to Israel as a volunteer.[11]

At the Third International Christian Zionist Congress held in Jerusalem under the auspices of the ICEJ, some 1,500 delegates from over forty countries unanimously affirmed 'The Lord in His zealous love for Israel and the Jewish People blesses and curses peoples and judges nations based upon their treatment of the Chosen People of Israel.'[12] Hal Lindsey makes similar claims: 'God has vowed, "He will bless those who bless Israel and curse those who curse her."'[13]

Cyrus Scofield and E. Schuyler English are largely responsible for popularizing this interpretation of Genesis 12:3 through the *Scofield Reference Bible* and its later editions. Notice how the footnotes in *The New Scofield Study Bible* 'enhance' Scofield's original notes (see Table 3.1).

Scofield Reference Bible	The New Scofield Study Bible
Wonderfully fulfilled in the history of the dispersion. It has invariably fared ill with the people who have persecuted the Jew – well with those who have protected him. The future will still more remarkably prove this principle.[14]	This was a warning literally fulfilled in the history of Israel's persecutions. It has invariably fared ill with the people who have persecuted the Jew – well with those who have protected him. For a nation to commit the sin of anti-Semitism brings inevitable judgment. The future will still more remarkably prove this principle.[15]

Table 3.1.

It is hard to see how God's promise to Abraham in Genesis 12:3 could possibly apply to his physical descendants today. It is true that the promise was reiterated by Abraham's son Isaac to his grandson Jacob in Genesis 27.

> May God give you of heaven's dew
>   and of earth's richness –
> an abundance of grain and new wine.
> May nations serve you
>   and peoples bow down to you.
> Be lord over your brothers,
>   and may the sons of your mother bow down to you.
> May those who curse you be cursed
>   and those who bless you be blessed.
> (Genesis 27:28–29)[16]

But here, as with the promise made to Abraham, it is a personal blessing. On this occasion Isaac is primarily concerned with Jacob's material needs and physical security in relation to his brothers.

So how do some commentators make the 4,000-year jump to apply Genesis 12 today? Scofield and Schuyler English look to Jesus' parable of the sheep and the goats in Matthew 25 and link this to their interpretation of Genesis 12. Once again, Schuyler English offers a more explicit application, favouring the nation of Israel while expunging Scofield's rather eccentric 'end-times' theology (see Table 3.2).

Scofield Reference Bible	The New Scofield Study Bible
... the persons judged are living nations ...	The subjects of this judgement are 'all nations' i.e. all Gentiles when living on earth.
three classes are present, sheep, goats, brethren ...	Three classes of individuals are mentioned: (1) sheep, saved Gentiles; (2) goats, unsaved Gentiles; and (3) brothers, the people of Israel ...
The test in this judgement is the treatment accorded by the nations to those whom Christ calls 'my brethren'. These 'brethren' are the Jewish Remnant who will have preached the Gospel of the kingdom to all nations during the tribulation.[17]	The test of this judgement is the treatment of individual Gentiles of those whom Christ calls 'brothers of mine' living in the preceding tribulation period when Israel is fearfully persecuted (cp. Gen. 12:3).[18]

Table 3.2.

Now there is just one small problem with this interpretation. It ignores earlier passages in Matthew where Jesus explains what he means by 'my brethren'. In Matthew 10, for example, Jesus describes the benefits of discipleship just before he sends out the apostles on their first training mission: 'And if anyone gives even a cup of cold water to one of these little ones who is known to be my disciple, truly I tell you, that person will certainly be rewarded' (Matthew 10:42). On another occasion, his mother and brothers are concerned for his welfare and come to take him home because they think 'He is out of his mind' (Mark 3:21). When he is told that they are outside the house asking for him, Jesus replies:

'Who is my mother, and who are my brothers?' Pointing to his disciples, he said, 'Here are my mother and my brothers. For whoever does the will of my Father in heaven is my brother and sister and mother.'

(Matthew 12:48–49)

Jesus clearly distinguished between his natural family and his spiritual family, as John emphasizes in the introduction to his Gospel (John 1:12–13). Jesus has defined 'his brethren' as those who trust and believe in him irrespective of their racial origins. It is therefore illegitimate to take a personal promise of divine blessing made to Abraham, to Jacob and then to ancient Israel and apply it in perpetuity to their descendants today. It is also irresponsible to suggest that God will bless us materially if we support the largely secular State of Israel, especially when this invariably means ignoring the plight of the indigenous Christian population of Palestine. The promise made to Abraham that the nations would be blessed through him was fulfilled in and through his 'seed', the Lord Jesus Christ (John 8:56; Galatians 3:16, 29).

So what is the relationship between Israel and the church? Who are God's chosen people? Let's go back to the Bible and examine the way 'Israel' is defined in the Old and New Testaments.

The Israel of God in the Old Testament
The myth of racial purity is nothing new, nor is the desire to limit or exclude those deemed inferior. This is particularly so today when defining Israel, since national identity tends to be restricted to those who are Jewish by race. Surprisingly perhaps, the Old Testament knows nothing of this contemporary form of nationalism known as Zionism. Instead, as we shall see, Israel as a nation was never narrowly restricted to those who were the physical descendants of the twelve sons of Jacob. Israel as a nation always incorporated people of other races, and this extended not just to their identity and right of residence but also to their inheritance of the land and right to worship God in the temple.

An inclusive Israel
Moses, for example, warned the Jewish people against a racial exclusivity:

Do not despise an Edomite, for the Edomites are related to you. Do not despise an Egyptian, because you resided as foreigners in their country.

The third generation of children born to them may enter the assembly of the Lord.
(Deuteronomy 23:7–8)

The Edomites, descended from Esau, lived in what is today the Negev and Southern Jordan. Similarly, King David looked forward to the day when other races – Egyptian (Rahab), Persian (Babylon), Palestinian (Philitia), Lebanese (Tyre) and African (Cush) – would have the same identity and privileges as the Israelites: 'I will record Rahab and Babylon among those who acknowledge me – Philistia too, and Tyre, along with Cush...' (Psalm 87:4). Notice the only criterion for citizenship that God lays down is faith. God welcomes all 'those who acknowledge me'. An inclusive Israel.

An inclusive inheritance

As if to emphasize that 'citizenship' means much more than a new passport, God instructs the Israelites to share the land and give an inheritance to all who trust in him.

'You are to allot it as an inheritance for yourselves and for the foreigners residing among you and who have children. You are to consider them as native-born Israelites; along with you they are to be allotted an inheritance among the tribes of Israel. In whatever tribe foreigners reside, there you are to give them their inheritance,' declares the Sovereign Lord.
(Ezekiel 47:22–23)

Those of other races, therefore, have the same rights as 'native Israelites'.

An inclusive temple

The inclusive nature of Israel extends beyond identity and inheritance to include the right to worship God in the temple. God declares through the prophet Isaiah his acceptance of all who come to him in faith.

Let no foreigners who have bound themselves to the Lord say,
'The Lord will surely exclude me from his people.' . . .

And foreigners who bind themselves to the LORD
   to minister to him,
to love the name of the LORD,
   and to be his servants,
all who keep the Sabbath without desecrating it
   and who hold fast to my covenant –
these I will bring to my holy mountain
   and give them joy in my house of prayer.
Their burnt offerings and sacrifices
   will be accepted on my altar;
for my house will be called
   a house of prayer for all nations.'
(Isaiah 56:3, 6–7)

Jesus cites Isaiah 56 to justify his actions in clearing the money changers and traders out of the temple. The religious leaders had turned the Court of the Gentiles into a noisy market, exploiting worshippers with inflated exchange rates and exorbitant prices for sacrifices.

The Israel of God in the New Testament

The inclusive nature of 'Israel' in the Old Testament is developed in the New Testament. Those who presumed that ancestry gave them certain religious privileges were chastened. John the Baptist's strong language indicates how seriously God viewed their pride and arrogance.

John said to the crowds coming out to be baptised by him, 'You brood of vipers! Who warned you to flee from the coming wrath? Produce fruit in keeping with repentance. And do not begin to say to yourselves, "We have Abraham as our father." For I tell you that out of these stones God can raise up children for Abraham. The axe has been laid to the root of the trees, and every tree that does not produce good fruit will be cut down and thrown into the fire.'
(Luke 3:7–9)

Jesus gives a similar warning to those who were trying to trap him. ' "Abraham is our father," they answered. "If you were Abraham's children," said Jesus, "then you would do what Abraham did" ' (John 8:39). Jesus goes even further in Matthew 8 when he praises the faith of a Gentile Roman centurion, 'Truly I tell you, I have not found anyone in Israel with such great faith' (Matthew 8:10). Jesus then goes on to make a prediction:

> I say to you that many will come from the east and the west, and will take their places at the feast with Abraham, Isaac and Jacob in the kingdom of heaven. But the subjects of the kingdom will be thrown outside, into the darkness, where there will be weeping and gnashing of teeth.
> (Matthew 8:11–12)

Here Jesus is warning his Jewish hearers that unless they recognize him as their Messiah they will be excluded from the kingdom.

This is how we are to understand Paul when he specifically uses the expression 'Israel of God' in Galatians 6:16. 'Peace and mercy to all who follow this rule, even to the Israel of God.' For Christian Zionists, Paul is referring to Jews, or at least Christian Jews, but this flies in the face of everything he has said in the first five chapters of this letter. In Galatians 1, Paul says we are saved by God's initiative – by his grace, and justified by faith alone in Jesus Christ. In chapters 2 – 3 Paul is emphatic – we are not saved by our racial pedigree, by circumcision, by offering animal sacrifices or by keeping the Law of Moses. In chapter 4, those who follow Jesus, as we shall see a little later, are likened to the free children of Sarah. Those seeking to be justified by the law have been alienated from Jesus and are likened to the children of Hagar. Quoting Genesis 21, they will, he warns, 'never share in the inheritance' (Galatians 4:30). In chapters 5 – 6, Paul speaks of our freedom in Christ and our new life in the Holy Spirit. He contrasts living by the Spirit with living by our sinful nature. In the closing verses of chapter 6, Paul summarizes the argument of the whole letter.

> Those who want to impress others by means of the flesh are trying to compel you to be circumcised. The only reason they do this is to avoid being persecuted for the cross of Christ. Not even those who are circumcised keep the law, yet they want you to be circumcised that they may boast about your circumcision in the flesh. May I never boast except in the cross of our Lord Jesus Christ, through which the world

has been crucified to me, and I to the world. Neither circumcision nor uncircumcision means anything; what counts is the new creation. Peace and mercy to all who follow this rule – to the Israel of God. From now on, let no-one cause me trouble, for I bear on my body the marks of Jesus. The grace of our Lord Jesus Christ be with your spirit, brothers and sisters. Amen.

(Galatians 6:12–18)

Do you see what Paul is saying? We have a choice: grace or law, faith or works? When Paul writes 'Peace and mercy to all who follow this rule – to the Israel of God' (Galatians 6:16), he is obviously referring to the followers of Jesus who have repudiated the legalists who wanted to impose circumcision and keeping the law. John Stott provides one of the best explanations of this verse:

> 'All who walk by this rule' and 'the Israel of God' are not two groups, but one. The connecting particle *kai* should be translated 'even', not 'and', or be omitted (as in RSV). The Christian church enjoys a direct continuity with God's people in the Old Testament. Those who are in Christ today are 'the true circumcision' (Phil. 3:3), 'Abraham's offspring' (Gal. 3:29) and 'the Israel of God'.[19]

And don't worry about the phrase 'walk by this rule' either. The Greek word translated 'rule' is *kanōn* and simply describes a carpenter's or surveyor's plumb line. John Stott says,

> This is the 'canon' of Scripture, the doctrine of the apostles, and especially in the context of Galatians 6 the cross of Christ and the new creation. Such is the rule by which the church must walk and continuously judge and reform itself.[20]

In the closing sentences of this letter, Paul is drawing on an ancient prayer he would have prayed all his life on the Sabbath. Known as the additional nineteenth benediction to the eighteen benedictions, and based on the Aaronic blessing of Numbers 6:24–26, God is asked in the final prayer for 'Peace . . . and mercy on us and all Israel, your people.' Now Paul prays this blessing on the Jewish and Gentile believers in Jesus, for they have become the 'Israel of God'.

As we have already seen from John 5:39, Jesus rebuked the Pharisees because they refused to acknowledge how the Hebrew Scriptures referred to him. Let us consider one example found in both the Old and New Testaments – the powerful imagery of the vine and vineyard.

The vine and the vineyard

The vine or vineyard is a symbol frequently associated with God's people in the Old Testament. Passages like Psalm 80, Isaiah 5, Jeremiah 2 and Hosea 10 provide the context for the way in which Jesus and his apostles invest the term with new and wider meaning. Drawing heavily on Isaiah 5, Jesus tells a parable in which God is likened to a landowner who plants a vineyard (see Table 3.3).

Isaiah 5:1–7	Matthew 21:33–41

I will sing for the one I love
    a song about his vineyard:
my loved one had a vineyard
    on a fertile hillside.
He dug it up and cleared it of stones
    and planted it with the choicest
        vines.
He built a watchtower in it
    and cut out a winepress as well.
Then he looked for a crop of good
        grapes,
    but it yielded only bad fruit.
 	
'Now you dwellers in Jerusalem and
        people of Judah,
    judge between me and my
        vineyard.
What more could have been done for
    my vineyard
    than I have done for it?
When I looked for good grapes,
    why did it yield only bad?
	'There was a landowner who planted
	a vineyard. He put a wall round it,
	dug a winepress in it and built a
	watchtower. Then he rented the
	vineyard to some farmers and moved
	to another place. When the harvest
	time approached, he sent his servants
	to the tenants to collect his fruit.
	
	'The tenants seized his servants;
	they beat one, killed another, and
	stoned a third. Then he sent other
	servants to them, more than the first
	time, and the tenants treated them in
	the same way. Last of all, he sent his
	son to them. "They will respect my
	son," he said.
	
	'But when the tenants saw the son,
	they said to each other, "This is the
	heir. Come, let's kill him and take his
	inheritance." So they took him and
	threw him out of the vineyard and
	killed him.

Now I will tell you
  what I am going to do to my
    vineyard:
I will take away its hedge,
  and it will be destroyed;
I will break down its wall,
  and it will be trampled.
I will make it a wasteland,
  neither pruned nor cultivated,
  and briers and thorns will grow
    there.
I will command the clouds
  not to rain on it.'

'Therefore, when the owner of the
vineyard comes, what will he do to
those tenants?'
  'He will bring those wretches to a
wretched end,' they replied, 'and he
will rent the vineyard to other
tenants, who will give him his share
of the crop at harvest time.'

The vineyard of the LORD Almighty
  is the house of Israel,
and the people of Judah
  are the vines he delighted in.
And he looked for justice, but saw
    bloodshed;
  for righteousness, but heard cries of
    distress.

Table 3.3.

In Matthew 21, Jesus takes the vivid imagery of Isaiah 5, and applies it specifically to himself. The failure of Israel to bear fruit is paralleled by the way the tenants treat the servants and ultimately the vineyard owner's son. Here, Jesus not only predicts his own death but warns that his Father will take the vineyard away from the Jewish leaders. 'Therefore I tell you that the kingdom of God will be taken away from you and given to a people who will produce its fruit' (Matthew 21:43).

This prophecy found its fulfilment in the Acts of the Apostles. At Pisidian Antioch, Luke records Paul warning them, 'We had to speak the word of God to you first. Since you reject it and do not consider yourselves worthy of eternal life, we now turn to the Gentiles' (Acts 13:46). The same thing occurred in Corinth. 'But when they [the Jews] opposed Paul and became abusive, he shook out his clothes in protest and said to them, "Your blood be on your own heads! I am innocent of it. From now on I will go to the Gentiles" ' (Acts 18:6). This is the basis for the view that the church, made up of both Jews and Gentiles, is the successor of the promises originally made to Israel.

John 15 is the most significant passage in the New Testament for understanding the analogy of the vine and the relationship between Israel and the church. When Jesus says 'I am the vine' he is making a very provocative statement. In the Old Testament, Israel is described as the vine (see for example, Jeremiah 11:16; Ezekiel 15:1–8; 17:1–10; Hosea 10:1–2; 14:6).

In Psalm 80, David uses the imagery of the vine to describe how God rescued the Israelites out of Egypt, 'planted it ... cleared the ground for it, and it took root and filled the land' (Psalm 80:8–9). But David goes on to describe how because of Israel's sin, 'Your vine is cut down, it is burned with fire; at your rebuke your people perish' (Psalm 80:16). At the same time David weaves in another analogy alongside that of the vine, which with hindsight, points to someone else beyond Israel:

> Watch over this vine,
>> the root your right hand has planted,
>> the son you have raised up for yourself.
> Your vine is cut down, it is burned with fire;
>> at your rebuke your people perish.
> Let your hand rest on the man at your right hand,
>> the son of man you have raised up for yourself.
> (Psalm 80:14–17)

Bruce Milne, in his helpful commentary on John 15, notes that 'Israel has failed God in the long-term role she was called to fulfil, that of being "a light for the Gentiles" (Is. 49:6), to bring God's salvation "to the ends of the earth".'[21]

> Israel, however, was more attracted by the gods of the surrounding nations than by her potential for penetrating them as a missionary ... But God's purpose, from which Israel turns in final apostasy, does not fall to the ground. It is grasped anew by the one who stands in the midst of Israel, and among the disciples. In contrast to the vine which

has destroyed itself by disobedience, Jesus is the 'true vine'. He is the
obedient Son through whose sacrifice and consequent mission the
age-old purpose of Israel would find fulfilment, the nations would be
reached, and 'all the families of the earth shall bless themselves'
(Gen. 12:3).[22]

Therefore, Jesus is the true vine, not Israel. He is the faithful Israelite
who will accomplish all that the nation of Israel failed to do. And in
this reinvigorated analogy, Jesus describes his followers as the living,
fruit-bearing branches of the vine. Remaining part of the vine and
bearing fruit depends on our abiding in Christ. Here Jesus is echoing
not only the language of Psalm 80 and Isaiah 5 but also that of John the
Baptist, who warned: 'The axe has been laid to the root of the trees,
and every tree that does not produce good fruit will be cut down and
thrown into the fire' (Matthew 3:10).

Similarly, Luke records how Peter uses the same imagery in his
sermon in Acts 3. Citing the words of Moses in Deuteronomy 18
concerning Jesus Christ, Peter warns: 'Anyone who does not listen to
him will be completely cut off from their people' (Acts 3:23).

The apostle Paul develops the analogy of the vine and branches
further in his letter to the Romans. In chapter 11 he explains the
relationship of the natural branches (Israel) to the wild branches
(Gentiles). His purpose is to curb any arrogance on the part of Gentile
believers:

> If some of the branches have been broken off, and you, though a wild
> olive shoot, have been grafted in among the others and now share in
> the nourishing sap from the olive root, do not consider yourself to be
> superior to those other branches. If you do, consider this: you do not
> support the root, but the root supports you. You will say then,
> 'Branches were broken off so that I could be grafted in.' Granted.
> But they were broken off because of unbelief, and you stand by faith.
> Do not be arrogant, but tremble. For if God did not spare the natural
> branches, he will not spare you either.
> (Romans 11:17–21)

Paul's use of the same analogy reinforces Jesus' own teaching in
John 15 (see Figure 3.2). In the following verses Paul offers the hope

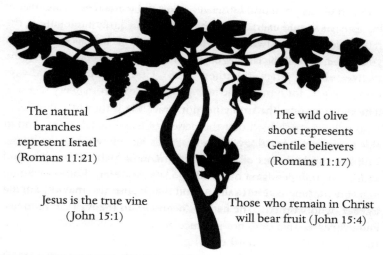

The natural
branches
represent Israel
(Romans 11:21)

The wild olive
shoot represents
Gentile believers
(Romans 11:17)

Jesus is the true vine
(John 15:1)

Those who remain in Christ
will bear fruit (John 15:4)

Figure 3.2. The vine and the branches.

that the Jewish people may once again be grafted in but only through faith in Jesus (Romans 11:22–24).

The New Testament does not teach that the Gentiles have superseded the Jews. But neither does it teach that the Jewish people retain a position of superiority over the Gentiles or over the church. There is continuity between the believers under the old covenant who looked forward to the coming of Christ and believers under the new covenant who look forward to his return. When Jesus died he broke down the wall of separation between Jew and Gentile.

> For he himself is our peace, who has made the two one and has destroyed the barrier, the dividing wall of hostility, by setting aside in his flesh the law with its commands and regulations. His purpose was to create in himself one new humanity out of the two, thus making peace, and in one body to reconcile both of them to God through the cross, by which he put to death their hostility.
> (Ephesians 2:14–16)

It is tragic that some appear to want to rebuild it. The Bible does not warrant a racial exclusivity giving any race preferential or elevated status in God's kingdom. However, Jesus did teach that in the future, his apostles would exert authority over Israel. 'Truly I tell you, at the renewal of all things, when the Son of Man sits on his glorious throne, you who have followed me will also sit on twelve thrones, judging the twelve tribes of Israel' (Matthew 19:28). God's intention has always been to create for himself one new people, drawn from every race and nation, under one head – the Lord Jesus Christ.

What then does it mean to be a Jew?

The apostle Paul once described himself as 'a Hebrew of Hebrews' and 'as for righteousness based on the law, faultless' (Philippians 3:5–6). He nevertheless refutes the notion that Jewishness may be defined by race or adherence to the Law of Moses. In his letter to the Romans, Paul explains:

> A person is not a Jew who is one only outwardly, nor is circumcision merely outward and physical. No, a person is a Jew who is one inwardly; and circumcision is circumcision of the heart, by the Spirit, not by the written code. Such a person's praise is not from other people, but from God.
> (Romans 2:28–29)

This is why a little later he says:

> For not all who are descended from Israel are Israel. Nor because they are his descendants are they all Abraham's children. On the contrary, 'It is through Isaac that your offspring will be reckoned.' In other words, it is not the natural children who are God's children, but it is the children of the promise who are regarded as Abraham's offspring.
> (Romans 9:6–8)

In his letter to the Philippians, Paul explicitly identifies the church as the true circumcision. 'For it is we who are the circumcision, we who serve God by his Spirit, who boast in Christ Jesus, and who put no confidence in the flesh' (Philippians 3:3). This is entirely consistent with the Old Testament, where, as we have already seen, citizenship of Israel was open to all 'those who acknowledge me' (Psalm 87:4). This is the same criterion found in the New Testament.

What does 'all Israel' mean?
Having identified the true Israel to be those who acknowledge Jesus as their Messiah, Paul can look forward to the day when, 'all Israel will be saved' (Romans 11:26). What does he mean? Well, there is a variety of possibilities. First, in context, what does Paul actually say?

I do not want you to be ignorant of this mystery, brothers and sisters, so that you may not think you are superior: Israel has experienced a hardening in part until the full number of the Gentiles has come in, and in this way all Israel will be saved. As it is written:

'The deliverer will come from Zion;
    he will turn godlessness away from Jacob.
And this is my covenant with them
    when I take away their sins.'

As far as the gospel is concerned, they are enemies for your sake; but as far as election is concerned, they are loved on account of the patriarchs, for God's gifts and his call are irrevocable. Just as you who were at one time disobedient to God have now received mercy as a result of their disobedience, so they too have now become disobedient in order that they too may now receive mercy as a result of God's mercy to you. For God has bound everyone over to disobedience so that he may have mercy on them all.
(Romans 11:25–32)

There are a number of possible ways to interpret this phrase 'all Israel will be saved'. Does Paul mean

1. all physical descendants of Abraham and Sarah living and resurrected when Jesus returns?
2. the remnant of Jews who believe in Jesus?
3. all descendants of Abraham and Sarah alive when God brings a national revival or Jesus returns?
4. all Jews and Gentiles together who believe in Jesus?

A common mistake, often made by those who favour the first option, is to assume Paul is saying 'And *then* all Israel will be saved', as if he is speaking chronologically. Scofield in his *Reference Bible*, for example, interprets the verse as promising a special role and status for national Israel after Jesus has returned and the church has been taken up into heaven. In a footnote to this verse he writes, 'According to the prophets, Israel, regathered from all nations, restored to her own land and converted, is yet to have her greatest earthly exaltation and glory.'[23] Dispensationalists, such as Lewis Sperry Chafer, John Walvoord and Arnold Fruchtenbaum, who believe God has two 'chosen' peoples – the church and Israel – argue that 'all Israel' refers to a 'national salvation' for the Jewish people, before, during or after Jesus returns.[24] This interpretation makes a special case for the Jews. It gives them a 'second chance' to be saved either because the Old Testament covenants are 'unconditional', because God will accept future animal sacrifices, or because a national revival will occur after Jesus returns and they see 'the one they have pierced' (Zechariah 12:10; see also John 19:37). However, none of these is taught in the New Testament. None of the passages referring to the return of Jesus give any hint of anyone being given a second chance. Hebrews 9 says 'Just as people are destined to die once, and after that to face judgment . . . ' (Hebrews 9:27). If judgment follows death, it is reckless as well as inconsistent to believe that God will treat Jews who are alive when Jesus returns any differently if they have, up to that point, rejected Jesus.

The TNIV helpfully translates the phrase 'in this way all Israel will be saved', meaning 'in this manner . . . '.[25] As we have seen, Paul has already defined what he means by 'Israel' earlier: 'For not all who are descended from Israel are Israel' (Romans 9:6). In narrowing his definition of 'Israel' to those who believe in Jesus, Paul has ruled out the first option. The term 'all Israel' cannot refer to those who have rejected, or will reject, Jesus, as they exclude themselves from the Israel of God.

Does Paul mean by 'all Israel', then, just a remnant of Jews who believe in Jesus, that is, those who are elect? The parallels with examples of how a 'remnant' was saved in the Old Testament are strong. God chose to save only a remnant during the exodus wilderness experience, on the slopes of Mount Sinai when the Law was given to Moses, and during the return from exile in Babylon. Those who perished, assimilated or apostatized were clearly not elect. Martyn Lloyd-Jones favours this position, interpreting 'all Israel' to mean 'the total of all believing Jews in all ages and generations'.[26] This view is shared by Louis Berkhof, for whom 'all Israel' refers to 'the whole number of the elect out of the ancient covenant people'.[27] The weakness of this position, if it may be considered as such, is that if Paul had intended us to understand only a remnant of Jews would ever be saved, he would have said so. It also misses the contrast Paul has created in the preceding verses. During the time of Gentile conversion, he has already told us that only a remnant of Jews will be saved, but when the full number of Gentiles has entered God's kingdom, then 'all Israel' will be saved. If a remnant is all that is hoped for in the future, where is the mystery in that (cf. Romans 11:25)?

So does Paul mean us to understand by 'all Israel' an 'end-time' revival of national proportions? John Stott notes that while Paul identifies the church as the 'Israel of God' in Galatians, here in Romans 'Israel' refers to national or ethnic Israel as opposed to the Gentiles. Therefore he offers another possibility:

> At present Israel is hardened except for a believing remnant, and will remain so until the Gentiles have come in. Then 'all Israel' must mean the great mass of Jewish people, comprising both the previously hardened majority and the believing minority.[28]

Agreeing with F. F. Bruce, Stott believes that the term does not mean 'every Jew without a single exception' but 'Israel as a whole'.[29] It is clear that in the Old Testament on occasions the phrase 'all Israel' simply means representatives of Israel, not every single Israelite, for example, in 2 Chronicles 5:3–4, where Solomon summons the elders of Israel to Jerusalem. Steve Motyer, in his comprehensive treatment of Romans 9 – 11, also favours this interpretation:

> The conversion of the last Gentile will be followed by a huge revival among the Jews, so that all Jews then alive will be ushered into the kingdom ... 'All Israel' in 11:26, I believe, is the entire company of those 'from the Jews' whom God wills to call 'my people', in fulfilment of his purposes of election.[30]

Leon Morris also notes the link between verses 25 and 26, 'and in this way' meaning just as a hardening on the part of Israel brought salvation to the Gentiles, when the full number of Gentiles have been saved, the temporary hardening of the Jews will come to an end and so 'the nation of Israel as a whole will ultimately have its place in God's salvation'.[31]

So is there any merit in the fourth option? John Calvin makes a good case:

> I extend the word *Israel* to include all the people of God in this sense, 'When the Gentiles have come in, the Jews will at the same time return from their defection to the obedience of faith. The salvation of the whole Israel of God, which must be drawn from both, will thus be completed, and yet in such a way that the Jews, as the first born in the family of God, may obtain the first place. I have thought that this interpretation is the more suitable, because Paul wanted here to point to the consummation of the kingdom of Christ, which is by no means confined to the Jews, but includes the whole world. In the same way, in Gal. 6:16, he calls the Church, which was composed equally of Jews and Gentiles, the Israel of God.[32]

In support of this position, Palmer Robertson observes that if in the preceding verse, 'the fullness of the Gentiles' refers to Gentile believers, he asks, 'into what do the full number of elect Gentiles come?':

> The answer is unavoidable. Believing Gentiles come *into Israel!* Is that not exactly the point made by Paul earlier in this chapter? Gentiles have been 'grafted in among' the Israel of God (Rom. 11:17). They have become additional branches, joined in the single stock that is none other than Israel ... In other words they have become 'Israelites.'[33]

This parallels Paul's arguments in Ephesians where he describes the Gentiles as 'separate from Christ, excluded from citizenship *in Israel* and foreigners to the covenants of the promise ... But now in Christ Jesus you who once were far away have been brought near by the blood of Christ' (Ephesians 2:12–13, emphasis added). Gentile believers are now, 'heirs together with Israel, members together of one body, and sharers together in the promise in Christ Jesus' (Ephesians 3:6). It is precisely this – the incorporation of Jews and Gentiles within Israel – that, as Paul says, constitutes the mystery of the gospel. So Palmer Robertson concludes: 'The full number that are the product of God's electing grace, coming from both the Jewish and the Gentile communities, will constitute the final Israel of God.'³⁴

That *Israel* now represents those who trust in Christ, both Jews and Gentiles, is made more explicit in Paul's letter to the Galatians. In Galatians 4, the well-known story of Abraham's two wives, Hagar and Sarah, is allegorized to illustrate the tensions between the Jewish legalists and the Christians in Galatia. The religious Jews insisted that their racial descent from Abraham gave them certain privileges over the Gentiles.

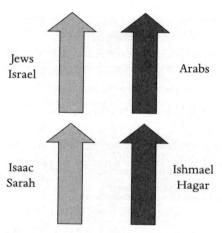

Figure 3.3. Natural descent through Abraham.

Controversially, Paul says that unbelieving Jews are the spiritual descendants of Hagar not Sarah, while the Galatian Christians are, like Isaac, the true children of promise (Galatians 4:21–28). Table 3.4 highlights the contrast Paul is making.

The promises made to Abraham, Isaac, Jacob and Joseph are therefore now fulfilled only through those who follow Jesus Christ, since they alone are designated the true children of Abraham and Sarah. Jews who reject Jesus Christ are outside the covenant of grace and are to be regarded as children of Hagar. Paul even takes Sarah's words of Genesis 21:10 and instructs the Galatian elders to eject the Judaizers who were corrupting the faith of the church in Galatia. 'Get rid of the slave woman and her son, for the slave woman's son will never share in the inheritance with the free woman's son' (Galatians 4:30).

Galatians	Unbelieving Jews	Jewish and Gentile Christians
4:22	Hagar	Sarah
	Slave woman	Free woman
4:23	Natural procreation	Supernatural promise
	Ishmael	Isaac
4:24–26	Mount Sinai	Jerusalem above
4:25	Earthly Jerusalem	Heavenly Jerusalem
4:28–30	Slavery	Freedom
4:29	Persecuting	Persecuted
4:30	Excluded from inheritance	Included in inheritance
4:31	Children of the slave woman	Children of the free woman

Table 3.4.

So the line of blessing is revealed to be spiritual or supernatural, rather than natural (see Figure 3.4). This is because legalism and grace, as means of gaining righteousness before God, are incompatible. And this is why, two chapters later, in summarizing his argument, Paul can describe God's new creation community of believing Jews and Gentiles as 'the Israel of God' (Galatians 6:16).

So which interpretation of 'all Israel' should we accept? As long as we believe 'there is no difference between Jew and Gentile', that

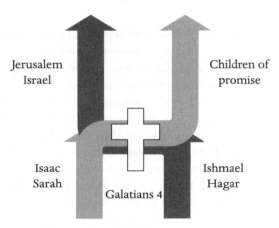

Figure 3.4. Spiritual descent through faith in Jesus.

'Everyone who calls on the name of the Lord will be saved' (Romans 10:12–13), believing God 'wants all people to be saved and to come to a knowledge of the truth' (1 Timothy 2:3), then perhaps we can accept whichever interpretation sounds most convincing and motivates us to love and good deeds.

What does it mean to be the 'chosen people'?
This understanding of Israel is enhanced by the way in which the Scriptures define the term 'chosen'. The first time the word is used it refers to God's promise to bless Abraham.

> Abraham will surely become a great and powerful nation, and all nations on earth will be blessed through him. For I have chosen him, so that he will direct his children and his household after him to keep the way of the LORD by doing what is right and just, so that the LORD will bring about for Abraham what he has promised him.
> (Genesis 18:18–19)

Abraham was chosen to lead his family to follow the Lord, so that his descendants would become a godly nation, and, through them, the whole world would be blessed. The promises made to Abraham were, however, conditional (Deuteronomy 7:6, 11–12; 8:1. See also Deuteronomy 14:2; Amos 3:1–2). The privilege of being 'chosen' clearly brought with it responsibility. They were 'chosen' for a purpose. The blessings promised were conditional on the faithfulness and obedience of God's people to make him known.

In Isaiah, the concept of 'chosenness' is applied principally to the coming Messiah, the Servant of the Lord. The universal nature of his role fulfils and supersedes that of Israel, for he will be a light to the Gentiles.

> It is too small a thing for you to be my servant
>   to restore the tribes of Jacob
>   and bring back those of Israel I have kept.
> I will also make you a light for the Gentiles,
>   that my salvation may reach to the ends of the earth.
> (Isaiah 49:6; see also Isaiah 42:6)

The coming Messiah is portrayed as the one who will fulfil the role that Israel has failed to. 'Here is my servant, whom I uphold, my chosen one in whom I delight; I will put my Spirit on him, and he will bring justice to the nations' (Isaiah 42:1). Note the contrast between the Servant of the Lord and servant Israel, who a few verses later are warned: 'Hear, you deaf; look, you blind, and see! Who is blind but my servant, and deaf like the messenger I send?' (Isaiah 42:18–19).

In his first public sermon, Jesus reads the prophecy given in Isaiah 61:1–2, and claims that it will be fulfilled in and through him (Luke 4:17–21). In Mark 13:20 Jesus clarifies that those who are 'chosen' are also known as the 'elect'. 'If the Lord had not cut short those days, no-one would survive. But for the sake of the elect, whom he has chosen, he has shortened them' (Mark 13:20). The apostle Peter similarly associates the two terms in the opening of his first epistle (1 Peter 1:1–2; see also 1 Peter 2:4). Here, Peter uses terminology associated with the Jewish *diaspora*, scattered as a consequence of the Assyrian and Babylonian exiles, and applies it to the church. Later in the same epistle, Peter describes the church as the chosen people of God (1 Peter 2:9–10).

Notice that Peter describes the church simply as God's people. The choice to translate this with a definite article in the English NIV translation expresses well the dramatic change that has come about for Gentiles who trust in Christ. As 'strangers in the world' with no formal identity, they are nevertheless 'elect', having 'been chosen according to the foreknowledge of God the Father . . .' (1 Peter 1:1–2). There is therefore no sense in which God has two separate peoples – the church and Israel. Jesus Christ is the 'Chosen One' (Luke 23:35, cf. Isaiah 42:1), and those who trust in him demonstrate that they are chosen also. Peter goes on to elaborate further:

> For you know that it was not with perishable things such as silver or gold that you were redeemed from the empty way of life handed down to you from your ancestors, but with the precious blood of Christ, a lamb without blemish or defect. He was chosen before the creation of the world, but was revealed in these last times for your sake . . .
>
> For in Scripture it says:

'See, I lay a stone in Zion,
   a chosen and precious cornerstone,
and the one who trusts in him
   will never be put to shame.'
  (1 Peter 1:18–20; 2:6)

'Chosenness' is therefore the sovereign act of God's grace, election and foreknowledge. It defines those who, by faith in Jesus Christ, are redeemed as children of God. The apostle Paul makes the same association in his letter to the Ephesians: 'In him we were also chosen, having been predestined according to the plan of him who works out everything in conformity with the purpose of his will' (Ephesians 1:11). In his letter to the Colossians, Paul emphasizes the inclusive nature of chosenness within the body of Christ:

> Here there is no Gentile or Jew, circumcised or uncircumcised, barbarian, Scythian, slave or free, but Christ is all, and is in all. Therefore, as God's chosen people, holy and dearly loved, clothe yourselves with compassion, kindness, humility, gentleness and patience.
> (Colossians 3:11–12)

In his letter to the Romans, Paul explains why the majority of Jewish people of his day, having rejected their Messiah, were now excluded from the covenant promises. However, as a sign that God has not rejected his people, Paul identifies himself with a 'remnant' of believing Jews, who are 'chosen by grace' and incorporated within the body of Christ (Romans 11:5).

Before the council in Jerusalem, Peter described how through signs and wonders God was drawing Gentiles to himself and 'did not discriminate between us and them' (Acts 15:9). James interprets this as the fulfilment of a prophecy of Amos (Amos 9:11–12).

> Simon has described to us how God first intervened to choose a people for his name from the Gentiles. The words of the prophets are in agreement with this, as it is written:

> 'After this I will return
>   and rebuild David's fallen tent.

> Its ruins I will rebuild,
>   and I will restore it,
> that the rest of humanity may seek the Lord,
>   even all the Gentiles who bear my name,
> says the Lord, who does these things' –
>   things known from long ago.

> It is my judgment, therefore, that we should not make it difficult for
> the Gentiles who are turning to God.
> (Acts 15:14–19)

Some claim that Amos is predicting the restoration of Israel as a nation. This is certainly not how James understands the prophecy. He says 'The words of the prophets are in agreement with this' – that is, with how God had supernaturally 'intervened to choose a people for his name among the Gentiles'. The context in which James cites Amos is entirely concerned with acknowledging that God was now choosing Gentiles as well as Jews to be his people. Both were saved equally by grace and without the necessity of circumcision or obedience to the law.

In the book of Revelation, John describes the ultimate security of those who trust in Jesus. 'They will make war against the Lamb, but the Lamb will triumph over them because he is Lord of lords and King of kings – and with him will be his called, chosen and faithful followers' (Revelation 17:14).

Significantly, the term 'chosen' is never used explicitly in the New Testament to refer to the Jewish people. It is used first of Jesus and then of all those who trust and believe in him, irrespective of nationality. Originally identified as the 'natural branches' and favoured because of the Patriarchs, the covenants, the law, temple worship and promises (Romans 9:1–4), the word 'chosen' has been invested with new meaning. It now means all who trust in Jesus Christ, irrespective of race.

What about the idea of a 'remnant'?
In Romans 11, Paul talks about a 'remnant chosen by grace' (Romans 11:5). Who are they and what does he mean? The idea of God saving a faithful remnant goes back to the story of Noah, where God rescues just one family from the flood (Genesis 7:23). The concept is picked up

again in the story of Joseph, who realizes why he has been elevated to high office in Egypt. 'But God sent me ahead of you to preserve for you a remnant on earth and to save your lives by a great deliverance' (Genesis 45:7). When Elijah thinks, 'I am the only one left' who is faithful (1 Kings 19:14), the Lord reveals that the remnant is actually much larger: 'Yet I reserve seven thousand in Israel – all whose knees have not bowed down to Baal' (1 Kings 19:18). Later in the history of the divided kingdom, the remnant becomes associated with just one tribe. 'So the LORD was very angry with Israel and removed them from his presence. Only the tribe of Judah was left . . .' (2 Kings 17:18). A little later the prophet Isaiah advises a rather discouraged King Hezekiah, 'Therefore pray for the remnant that still survives' (2 Kings 19:4). Just before his prediction of the birth of Immanuel, the Messiah, Isaiah promises, 'though a tenth remains in the land, it will again be laid waste. But as the terebinth and oak leave stumps when they are cut down, so the holy seed will be the stump in the land' (Isaiah 6:13). God's people will, he promises, grow again through 'the holy seed'. Significantly, Jesus quotes the preceding verses (Isaiah 6:9–10) to explain why the unbelieving crowds will not understand his parable of the farmer's seed. Only those who 'hear the word' and 'accept it' will 'produce a crop – some thirty, some sixty, some a hundred times what was sown' (Mark 4:1–20). And here we have the hint that, under the new covenant, the small remnant will grow. Isaiah says as much a little later in his prophecy of judgment and restoration (Isaiah 10:17–22).

Notice the size of the remnant, 'so few a child could write them down'; and the place of return – first of all, 'to the Mighty God'. After the restoration from exile, Ezra can give thanks, 'But now, for a brief moment, the LORD our God has been gracious in leaving us a remnant and giving us a firm place in his sanctuary . . .' (Ezra 9:8), though still as 'slaves' because of their sin (Ezra 9:9–15).

At the birth of Jesus, the remnant is made up of a few people like Simeon and Anna, who praise God when they recognize the child as the one who will be 'a light for revelation to the Gentiles, and the glory of your people Israel' (Luke 2:25–38). Jesus specifically chose twelve apostles (Mark 3:16–19) to take the good news, first to the lost sheep of Israel (Matthew 10:5–6; 15:24).

But at his death, how many were left in that remnant? The short answer is 'none'. At his arrest in Gethsemane, Matthew tells us, 'Then all the disciples deserted him and fled' (Matthew 26:56). Even Peter disowns Jesus when challenged (Luke 22:54–62). In his death, it may be said that the 'remnant of Israel' has been reduced to one man. As Isaiah anticipates, 'We all, like sheep, have gone astray, each of us has turned to our own way; and the LORD has laid on him the iniquity of us all' (Isaiah 53:6). When Jesus died, we were, says Paul, 'God's enemies' (Romans 5:10). So Jesus was in his life, and supremely in his death, the remnant of Israel.

So, in reviewing the promise made to Abraham that 'all peoples on earth will be blessed through you' (Genesis 12:3), and that his descendants would be like the stars in the sky and the sand on the seashore (Genesis 22:17), the apostle Paul could now understand these as fulfilled in and through Jesus Christ. 'The promises were spoken to Abraham and to his seed. Scripture does not say "and to seeds", meaning many people, but "and to your seed", meaning one person, who is Christ' (Galatians 3:16). From the cross onwards, membership of the 'remnant' is now limited to those who identify with this 'seed' which is Christ. The apostle John writes,

He came to that which was his own, but his own did not receive him. Yet to all who did receive him, to those who believed in his name, he gave the right to become children of God – children born not of natural descent, nor of human decision or a husband's will, but born of God. (John 1:11–13)

At Pentecost, the 'remnant' of eleven restored disciples, together with the family of Jesus, is, through the preaching of the cross, supernaturally enlarged to three thousand (Acts 2:41), a number the Lord adds to daily (Acts 2:47), and soon grows to five thousand (Acts 4:4). In the book of Revelation the remnant now includes '144,000 from all the tribes of Israel' and 'a great multitude that no-one could count, from every nation, tribe, people and language, standing before the throne' (Revelation 7:4–10).

A helpful way to visualize this remnant and its shape through history, from the promise made to Abraham to its fulfillment and realization in heaven, is to think of an hourglass (see Figure 3.5).

This is how we should understand Paul's statement in Romans 11:5. The remnant are 'chosen by grace'. He goes on to spell out the

Promise to Abraham	Genesis 12:3; 22:17
The remnant of Judah	2 Kings 17
The remnant of Exiles	Isaiah 6:13; 10:20; Ezra 9:9–15
Jesus the 'seed' remnant	Isaiah 53; Galatians 3:16
The apostolic remnant	Acts 1:12–14
The pentecost church	John 1:12–13; Acts 2:41, 44
The great multitude	Revelation 7:4–10

Figure 3.5. The remnant hourglass – from promise to fulfilment.

consequences. 'And if by grace, then it cannot be based on works; if it were, grace would no longer be grace' (Romans 11:6).

So who are the real 'children of God'?

While the majority of Jewish people of Jesus' generation rejected him, all who did receive him as their Lord and Saviour, irrespective of their race, were the legitimate heirs of the covenant promises. The apostle John explains this at the beginning of his Gospel where he states that those who receive Jesus are the 'children of God'.

> He came to that which was his own, but his own did not receive him. Yet to all who did receive him, to those who believed in his name, he gave the right to become children of God – children born not of natural descent, nor of human decision or a husband's will, but born of God. (John 1:11–13)

In Acts 3, the apostle Peter explains to the many nationalities present in Jerusalem how the death of Jesus was no accident but the sovereign will of God, foretold by Moses and the prophets, and the sole means by which all people can be reconciled to God (Acts 3:24–26). Significantly, Peter says that those who trust in Jesus are the 'heirs of the prophets and of the covenant' (Acts 3:25). He sees the promises made to Abraham fulfilled not through national Israel but through the church.

In Paul's letter to the Ephesians, we are given a glorious insight into how Jewish and Gentile believers in Jesus Christ have been brought into a new 'citizenship' (Ephesians 2:11–16).

The 'dividing wall of hostility', typified by the barrier that separated Jews and Gentiles in the temple, has been broken down by Jesus Christ.

It is ironic, if tragic, that despite his willingness to comply with all the petty temple regulations concerning ritual purity, Paul would eventually be arrested for allegedly bringing Greeks into the temple and defiling God's house (Acts 21:28–29). Today, their successors in the government of Israel are seeking to erect a much higher and longer 'separation barrier' to preserve their racial identity and exclusive claim to the land of Palestine.

Paul goes on to show how, having broken down the wall of partition, Jesus has created a new living temple made up of people of all races (Ephesians 2:19–22). Paul cites the prophet Hosea as evidence that this new inclusive understanding of God's people has always been God's intention and sovereign will (Romans 9:21–26, see Hosea 1:10; 2:23).

The incorporation of both Jews and Gentiles into the one people of God is further illustrated by the way the writer to the Hebrews understands the continuity and unity between the saints of the Old Testament church and the saints of the New Testament church. In Hebrews 11, we find a catalogue of the Old Testament saints and how they suffered for their faith. The chapter concludes with this summary:

> These were all commended for their faith, yet none of them received what had been promised. God had planned something better for us so that only together with us would they be made perfect.
> (Hebrews 11:39–40)

Notice that the writer says 'only *together with us* would they be made perfect'. This is because the Old Testament saints, saved by faith as we are, could only hope for their salvation. They cannot experience their inheritance in its fullest sense until the Lord Jesus dies in their place and the dead in Christ are raised (1 Thessalonians 4:16). Then, and only then, will, 'we who are still alive and are left will be caught up together with them in the clouds to meet the Lord in the air. And so we will be with the Lord for ever' (1 Thessalonians 4:17). Notice here, Paul uses the expression '*together with them*'. This is why Jesus could say, 'Abraham rejoiced at the thought of seeing my day; he saw it and was glad' (John 8:56). The church of Jesus Christ therefore brings 'together' in a unity of faith and love his children under the old and new covenants, Jews and Gentiles who trust and believe in Jesus –

the one looking forward, the other looking back to his first coming and upward for his second.

Finally, in the vision which God gave the apostle John, we see the church as she is becoming in all her radiant glory.

> After this I looked, and there before me was a great multitude that no-one could count, from every nation, tribe, people and language, standing before the throne and in front of the Lamb. They were wearing white robes and were holding palm branches in their hands. (Revelation 7:9)

This is why it is inappropriate to maintain racial distinctions within the body of Christ, or claim the Jewish people have a separate relationship with God based on their ancestry or Mosaic Law. The promises made to the Patriarchs and Israel are now being fulfilled in and through the church. We must therefore not erect once again a wall of separation that Jesus has broken down by his death in our place (Ephesians 2:14).

It is very revealing to compare words used in the Old Testament to describe Israel and see how the New Testament applies them to the church. Table 3.5 gives a few examples:

Israel: The church in the Old Testament	The body of Christ: The church in the New Testament
Righteous live by faithfulness (Habakkuk 2:4)	Righteous live by faith (Romans 1:17)
Holy people (Deuteronomy 7:6; 33:3; (Numbers 16:3)	Holy people (Ephesians 1:1; Romans 1:7)
Chosen (Deuteronomy 7:6; 14:2)	Chosen (Colossians 3:12; Titus 1:1)
Loved (Deuteronomy 4:37)	Loved (Colossians 3:12; 1 Thessalonians 1:4)
Called (Isaiah 41:9; 2 Chronicles 7:14)	Called (Romans 1:6–7; 1 Corinthians 1:2)

Assembly (Psalms 1:5; 89:5; 149:1)	Assembly (Acts 7:38; 20:28; Hebrews 2:12)
'Church' = Assembly in Greek OT (Micah 2:5)	Church (Matthew 16:18; 18:17; Ephesians 2:20)
Flock (Ezekiel 34:2, 7; Psalm 77:20)	Flock (Luke 12:32; Acts 20:28)
Holy nation (Exodus 19:6)	Holy nation (1 Peter 2:9)
Treasured possession (Exodus 19:5)	Special possession (1 Peter 2:9)
Kingdom of priests (Exodus 19:6)	Royal priesthood (1 Peter 2:9)
Children of God (Hosea 1:10)	Children of God (John 1:12)
People of God (Hosea 2:23)	People of God (1 Peter 2:10)
People of his inheritance (Deuteronomy 4:20)	Glorious inheritance (Ephesians 1:18)
My dwelling place = tabernacle (Leviticus 26:11; Ezekiel 37:27)	Dwelling among us = tabernacle (John 1:14; 2 Corinthians 6:16)
I will walk among you (Leviticus 26:12; Jeremiah 32:38)	I will ... walk among them (2 Corinthians 6:16–17)
I will be his father = of David (2 Samuel 7:14)	I will be a father to you (2 Corinthians 6:18)
God is a husband betrothed (Isaiah 54:5; Jeremiah 3:14; 31:32; Hosea 2:19)	Christ is a husband betrothed (2 Corinthians 11:2; Ephesians 5:25–30)
Twelve tribes (Genesis 49:28; Revelation 21:12)	Twelve apostles (Mark 3:14; Revelation 21:14)

Table 3.5.

As we have seen, the biblical imagery of the vineyard, the vine and the branches, as well as terms such as the 'Israel of God' and 'chosenness', point to the inclusive nature of God's new creation community. Through faith, and faith in Jesus Christ alone, we become children of God, members of the one and only, truly international Israel of God.

Chapter summary points

- God has only ever had one people.
- Citizenship of Israel was always open to all people who acknowledged God.
- Old Testament analogies for Israel are applied in the New Testament to the church.
- God's people have always been inclusive and spiritual, not exclusive and physical.
- The promises made to Abraham are fulfilled in and through the church.
- Those who receive Jesus as their Lord and Saviour are:

> Branches in the vine
> Brethren of Jesus
> Chosen people
> The remnant
> Children of God
> Children of Abraham and Sarah
> The Israel of God

Passages to review
John 15; Ephesians 2; Galatians 4; Romans 2; 9 – 11.

Questions for further study

1. Why are the followers of Jesus described as God's 'chosen people'?
2. Which of the Old Testament analogies for Israel applied to the church in the New Testament do you find most meaningful and why?
3. What exactly was the 'wall of separation' that Jesus has broken down?
4. How did he remove it and why?
5. In what sense was the 'remnant of Israel' reduced to one man as Jesus died on the cross?
6. How does the idea of a remnant evolve and develop in Scripture?
7. In the light of this, how should we regard Jewish people today?

The Promised Land: From the Nile to
4. the Euphrates?

Those who insist that the Jewish people are God's 'chosen people' also insist that the promises made to Abraham and the Patriarchs, concerning the land bequeathed to them, are promises that apply to his physical descendants today. So the contemporary State of Israel is seen as evidence of God's continuing protection and favour toward the Jewish people. David Brickner sees the occupation of Palestine in 1948 and Jerusalem in 1967 as the fulfilment of the promises made to Abraham and the Patriarchs:

> I believe the modern day state of Israel is a miracle of God and
> a fulfilment of Bible prophecy. Jesus clearly said that 'Jerusalem
> would be trodden down by the Gentiles until the time of the nations
> is fulfilled' (Luke 21:24). It has been 50 years since the founding of
> that state, but only 30 years since Jerusalem came under the control
> of Jews for the first time since Jesus made that prediction. Could it
> be that 'this generation shall not pass until all these things are
> fulfilled?'[1]

So, the Third International Christian Zionist Congress held in Jerusalem in 1996 expressed the belief of many in affirming:

According to God's distribution of nations, the Land of Israel has been given to the Jewish People by God as an everlasting possession by an eternal covenant. The Jewish People have the absolute right to possess and dwell in the Land, including Judea, Samaria, Gaza and the Golan.[2]

In this chapter we will consider what the Bible has to say about the significance and purposes of the Promised Land, as well as its geographical extent. Then we will look at whether the land was intended as an 'everlasting possession' of the Jewish people or whether they were only ever temporary residents. We will go on to examine the terms under which they were allowed to return after the exile, and whether the kingdom was nationalistic or universal. Finally, we must consider what Jesus and the apostles have to say about all this.

The significance and purposes of the Promised Land
In God's redemptive plan he chose Abram, from what is today Iraq, and called him to leave his home in Ur by the Euphrates and go to the land of Canaan. These were the promises God made:

The LORD had said to Abram, 'Go from your country, your people and your father's household to the land I will show you.

  'I will make you into a great nation,
     and I will bless you;
  I will make your name great,
     and you will be a blessing.
  I will bless those who bless you,
     and whoever curses you I will curse;
  and all peoples on earth
     will be blessed through you.'

  So Abram left, as the LORD had told him.
(Genesis 12:1–4)

After Ishmael was born to Abram and Hagar, God ratified the covenant once more (Genesis 17:1–8).

The covenant promises made to Abraham were repeated again after Isaac was born (Genesis 22:16–18). They were subsequently made to Isaac 'because Abraham obeyed me' (Genesis 26:2–5), and then finally to his grandson Jacob (Genesis 28:13–15). There is no doubt that the vision of a 'Promised Land' was central to the hopes and aspirations of God's people as they languished in slavery in Egypt, as well as during their long wanderings through the wilderness of Sinai (Exodus 23:27–33). The promise of land with specific boundaries demonstrated the trustworthiness of God and his faithfulness in caring for those who called upon his name (See Genesis 26:3–5; Exodus 6:1–8; Joshua 24:11–27). God's faithfulness in the land promises was celebrated throughout the history of Israel, notably in Psalm 105.

> [Y]ou his servants, the descendants of Abraham,
>   his chosen ones, the children of Jacob.
> He is the LORD our God;
>   his judgments are in all the earth.
> He remembers his covenant for ever,
>   the promise he made, for a thousand generations,
> the covenant he made with Abraham,
>   the oath he swore to Isaac.
> He confirmed it to Jacob as a decree,
>   to Israel as an everlasting covenant:
> 'To you I will give the land of Canaan
>   as the portion you will inherit.'
> (Psalm 105:6–11; see also verses 37–45)

Clearly, the covenants were intended to instil trust in God and faithful obedience from his people. Yet, the present ambiguous borders of Israel are only a fraction of those God apparently intended for the Jewish people.

The geographical boundaries of Israel: from Egypt to Iraq?

The boundaries of the land God promised to Abraham and his descendants are demarcated in Genesis 15. 'On that day the LORD made a covenant with Abram and said, "To your descendants I give this land, from the river of Egypt to the great river, the Euphrates"' (Genesis 15:18). The 'river of Egypt' most likely refers to one of the tributaries of the Nile. The word in Hebrew, *nāhār*, denotes a large river, and this is how early Aramaic translations along with Jewish commentaries identify the location (see 1 Chronicles 13:5). The Euphrates begins in Turkey and flows through Syria and Iraq before entering the Persian Gulf.

If these boundaries were applied today, and depending on the route of the southern border from Eilat to the Euphrates, parts of Egypt, Lebanon, Syria, Jordan, Palestine, Iraq, and even Kuwait and parts of Saudi Arabia would be incorporated. Some Zionist groups lay claim to all this territory using the term 'Eretz Israel HaShlema' to denote the whole or complete land of Israel. While most secular Israelis today would not identify with these 'biblical' borders, the founders of Zionism, including Theodore Herzl, Vladimir Jabotinsky and David Ben-Gurion, certainly did (see Figure 4.1). They saw the creation of the Hashemite Kingdom of Transjordan, in 1922, as a betrayal of the British Mandate because it denied Zionists the right to settle there.

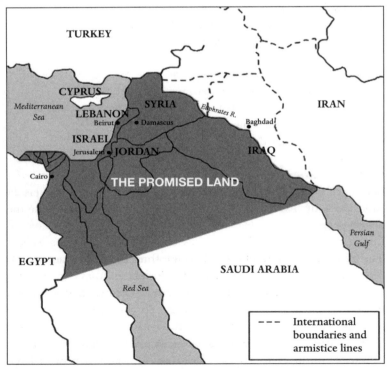

Figure 4.1. The Israel of Theodore Herzl (1904) and of Rabbi Fischmann (1947).

Nevertheless, it is significant that after nearly sixty years since the foundation of the State of Israel, successive governments have failed to declare what they regard as their territorial boundaries. Israel must be the only country in the world that has not yet recognized its own borders.

Cyrus Scofield, in a footnote to Deuteronomy 30:5 in his *Reference Bible*, claims 'It is important to see that the nation has never as yet taken the land under the unconditional Abrahamic covenant nor has it ever possessed the whole land.'[3] Arnold Fruchtenbaum elaborates further on why this claim to much of the Middle East is non-negotiable.

> So, then, according to the Scriptures, three promises are made with regard to the land: first, Abraham, Isaac, and Jacob were all promised the possession of the land; second, the descendants of Abraham, Isaac, and Jacob were promised the possession of the land; and third, the boundaries of the promised land extended from the Euphrates River in the north to the River of Egypt in the south ... At no point in Jewish history have the Jews ever possessed all of the land from the Euphrates in the north to the River of Egypt in the south. Since God cannot lie, these things must yet come to pass. Somehow or other, Abraham, Isaac, and Jacob must possess all the land, and second, the descendants of Abraham must settle in all of the promised land.[4]

The problem with this kind of literalism is that it goes too far, setting Scripture against Scripture. Advocates have to ignore the way the Bible itself interprets the promises made to Abraham, Isaac and Jacob. The books of Joshua, 1 Kings and Nehemiah all indicate that the promises were fulfilled. Having entered Canaan, the Bible tells us, 'So Joshua took the entire land, just as the LORD had directed Moses' (Joshua 11:23). At the end of the book of Joshua, the same assessment is repeated but rather more emphatically (Joshua 21:43–45).

However, in chapter 23, in Joshua's farewell address before he dies, he says:

> Remember how I have allotted as an inheritance for your tribes all the land of the nations that remain – the nations I conquered – between the Jordan and the Mediterranean in the west. The LORD your God himself

will push them for your sake. He will drive them out before you, and you will take possession of their land, as the LORD your God promised you. (Joshua 23:4–5)

Clearly Joshua and the Israelites did not conquer all the territory and yet he believed 'Not one of all the LORD's good promises to the house of Israel failed; every one was fulfilled' (Joshua 21:45). So either the writer of Joshua was not a 'literalist' in the modern sense of the word, or perhaps he had the wrong maps.

In 2 Samuel, the writer describes how King David 'went to restore his control along the Euphrates River' (2 Samuel 8:3–4), suggesting that, even if only briefly, the kingdom had by then extended this far north. Then under King Solomon, the boundaries of Israel were consolidated, extending from Egypt to the Euphrates. The writer of 1 Kings uses the metaphor of sand on the seashore from Genesis 22:17 to show that he understood the boundaries of Solomon's kingdom to be a fulfilment of the promises made to Abraham (1 Kings 4:20–21, 24). Tiphsah, mentioned in this passage, was a city on the west bank of the Euphrates. By around 440 BC Nehemiah could look back and give thanks to God for the fulfilment of his promises, again using the language of Genesis (Nehemiah 9:7–9, 25).

It is hard to see how these clear statements, which demonstrate the faithfulness of God, can be ignored or reconciled with the ultra-literalist claims of those who insist the promises have yet to be fulfilled.

Everlasting possession or conditional residence?
The land of Canaan was given to the Israelites as a sign of God's grace and mercy, not because of their size or significance (Deuteronomy 7:7). Nor was the land a reward for their righteousness or integrity. In fact, God describes them in rather less than complimentary terms as a 'stiff-necked people' (Deuteronomy 9:5–6). Moses and the Hebrew prophets repeatedly state that the land belongs to God and residence there is always conditional. For example, 'The land must not be sold permanently, because the land is mine and you reside in my land as foreigners and strangers' (Leviticus 25:23).

In Jeremiah 2, God says, 'I brought you into a fertile land to eat its fruit and rich produce. But you came and defiled *my* land and made *my* inheritance detestable' (Jeremiah 2:7, emphasis added). It is God's land not theirs (see also Jeremiah 16:18). Because the land belongs to God, it cannot be permanently bought or sold. The land is never at the disposal of Israel for its own purposes. Instead it is Israel who is at God's disposal. The Jews remain foreigners and strangers in God's land. Perhaps this is why it is only referred to as the 'land of Israel' six times in the whole of the Bible. The reason is clear. It is God's land, as is the rest of the earth (Psalm 24:1).

Zionists, however, like to emphasize that God promised the land from Egypt to Iraq as an 'everlasting possession' (Genesis 17:8). So the International Christian Embassy says:

> We simply believe the Bible. And that Bible, which we understand has not been revoked, makes it quite clear that God has given this land as an eternal inheritance to the Jewish people … According to God's distribution of nations, the Land of Israel has been given to the Jewish People by God as an everlasting possession by an eternal covenant. The Jewish People have the absolute right to possess and dwell in the Land, including Judea, Samaria, Gaza and the Golan.[5]

They therefore invariably oppose the dismantling of Jewish settlements in Gaza and the Occupied Territories, justify the Separation Barrier, assist Jewish people from around the world to move to Israel, and support the colonization of Palestine. Exobus is just one of many organizations funding the transportation of Jews to Israel,[6] while Christian Friends of Israeli Communities actively encourage churches to adopt and fund illegal Jews-only Settlements in the Occupied Territories.[7]

Genesis 17:8 does indeed describe the land as an 'everlasting possession'. However, a text without a context is a pretext, and Genesis 17:8 is a good example. The very next verse provides the context in the form of a conditional clause.

> Then God said to Abraham, 'As for you, you must keep my covenant, you and your descendants after you for the generations to come' …
> Any uncircumcised male, who has not been circumcised in the flesh, will be cut off from his people; he has broken my covenant.
> (Genesis 17:9, 14)

Residence in the land was therefore always conditional. In Deuteronomy, residence in the land is explicitly made conditional on adherence to the law. Notice the 'if' and 'because':

> If the LORD your God enlarges your territory, as he promised on oath to your ancestors, and gives you the whole land he promised them, because you carefully follow all these laws I command you today – to love the LORD your God and to walk always in obedience to him ...
> (Deuteronomy 19:8–9)

At the end of Deuteronomy, God promises his people blessings for obedience and curses for disobedience (see Table 4.1).

Blessings for obedience	Curses for disobedience
If you fully obey the LORD your God and carefully follow all his commands that I give you today, the LORD your God will set you high above all the nations on earth. All these blessings will come on you and accompany you if you obey the LORD your God... The LORD will grant that the enemies who rise up against you will be defeated before you. They will come at you from one direction but flee from you in seven... Then all the peoples on earth will see that you are called by the name of the LORD, and they will fear you. (Deuteronomy 28:1–3, 7, 10)	However, if you do not obey the LORD your God and do not carefully follow all his commands and decrees I am giving you today, all these curses will come on you and overtake you: You will be cursed in the city and cursed in the country... The LORD will cause you to be defeated before your enemies. You will come at them from one direction but flee from them in seven... You will be uprooted from the land you are entering to possess. Then the LORD will scatter you among all nations, from one end of the earth to the other. (Deuteronomy 28:15–16, 25, 63–64)

Table 4.1.

In Leviticus, the language is even more explicit, leaving no room for doubt. Even while the Israelites were still wandering in the desert, the Lord uses some of the most graphic language in the Bible to spell out the basis for their future residency in the Promised Land (Leviticus 18:24–28).

The opening chapter of Joshua provides a good example of the promises and conditions given to the Israelites as they are about to enter Canaan (see Table 4.2).

Unconditional promise	Conditional clause
Get ready to cross the River Jordan into the land I am about to give to them – to the Israelites. I will give you every place where you set your foot, as I promised Moses. Your territory will extend from the desert to Lebanon, and from the great river, the Euphrates – all the Hittite country – to the Mediterranean Sea in the west. No-one will be able to stand against you all the days of your life. (Joshua 1:2–5)	Be careful to obey all the law my servant Moses gave you; do not turn from it to the right or to the left, that you may be successful wherever you go. Keep this Book of the Law always on your lips; meditate on it day and night, so that you may be careful to do everything written in it. Then you will be prosperous and successful. (Joshua 1:7–8)

Table 4.2.

As the conquest begins, we find by Joshua 7 the Israelites are threatened not just with exile but with destruction.

Israel has sinned; they have violated my covenant, which I commanded them to keep. They have taken some of the devoted things; they have stolen, they have lied, they have put them with their own possessions. That is why the Israelites cannot stand against their enemies; they turn their backs and run because they have been made liable to destruction. I will not be with you any more unless you destroy whatever among you is devoted to destruction.
(Joshua 7:11–12)

Notice the conditional clause, 'I will not be with you . . . unless . . .' So, the unconditional promises concerning the land were always clarified or supplemented by conditional clauses. These made continued residence in the land dependent on adherence to the covenant terms. Near the end of Joshua's final speech he repeats the warning:

> If you violate the covenant of the LORD your God, which he commanded you, and go and serve other gods and bow down to them, the LORD's anger will burn against you, and you will quickly perish from the good land he has given you.
> (Joshua 23:16)

The warnings of the prophets, in explaining the reasons for their exile from the land, reinforce the promises and warnings of the Mosaic Law. Jeremiah 7 is just one example: 'Through your own fault you will lose the inheritance I gave you. I will enslave you to your enemies in a land you do not know, for you have kindled my anger, and it will burn for ever' (Jeremiah 7:4).

Thankfully God's anger did not literally 'burn for ever' against the Jewish people, because he sent Jesus to take their punishment and ours upon himself (Isaiah 53:4–6). The pattern set in the Law and Prophets is nevertheless one tested by the existence of a largely secular State of Israel.

Repentance, revival and restoration: but in which order?

From their beginnings in the early decades of the nineteenth century, organizations such as the London Jews' Society promoted the belief that the Jewish people would come to recognize Jesus as their Messiah, be restored to the land once more, and then Jesus would return. Scofield claimed that biblical prophecies foretold a third restoration to the land coinciding with the return of Jesus: 'Israel is now in the third dispersion from which she will be restored at the return of the Lord as King under the Davidic Covenant.'[8] Until the beginning of the twentieth century, the consensus was that God would restore the Jewish people to Palestine as a Christian nation.

With the birth of the Zionist movement, and growing numbers of secular Jews emigrating to Palestine, Christian writers began to seek an alternative prophetic interpretation. E. Schuyler English, who supervised the revision of the *Scofield Reference Bible* in 1967, adds the following footnote to Deuteronomy 30:5 which is absent from Scofield's original: '... when the nation walked in conformity with the will of God, it enjoyed the blessing and protection of God. In the twentieth century the exiled people began to be restored to their homeland.'[9] In the 1984 edition the wording was revised yet again to read: 'In the twentieth century the exiled people were restored to their homeland.'[10]

Conveniently, the vision of the 'dry bones' in Ezekiel 37 seemed to explain what was happening. Hal Lindsey offers this interpretation, adding capitals for emphasis, in case you miss the plot:

> Ezekiel 37:7–8 ... is phase one of the prophecy which predicts the PHYSICAL RESTORATION of the Nation without Spiritual life which began May 14, 1948 ... Ezekiel 37:9–10 ... is phase two of the prophecy which predicts the SPIRITUAL REBIRTH of the nation AFTER they are physically restored to the land as a nation ... The Lord identifies the bones in the allegory as representing 'the whole house of Israel.' It is crystal clear that this is literally predicting the restoration and rebirth of the whole nation at the time of Messiah's coming [Ezekiel 37:21–27].[11]

Charles Spurgeon called this kind of dodgy interpretation 'exegesis by current events',[12] for interpreting Scripture in the light of history rather than the other way round. Mocking the speculations of some of his contemporaries he wrote,

> Your guess at the number of the beast, your Napoleonic speculations, your conjectures concerning a personal Antichrist – forgive me, I count them but mere bones for dogs; while men are dying, and hell is filling, it seems to me the veriest drivel to be muttering about an Armageddon at Sebastopol or Sadowa or Sedan, and peeping between the folded leaves of destiny to discover the fate of Germany.[13]

In this instance, Lindsey and others have reversed the clear and unambiguous process outlined in the promises and warnings of the Law and Prophets who teach that repentance leads to restoration, not the other way round. It is hard to see how this novel interpretation of

Ezekiel can be reconciled with the warnings given just a few chapters earlier. In Ezekiel 33, it seems that the Lord anticipated the reasoning of those who arrogantly claimed rights to the land because of the promise made originally to Abraham:

> Son of man, the people living in those ruins in the land of Israel are saying, 'Abraham was only one man, yet he possessed the land. But we are many; surely the land has been given to us as our possession.'
> Therefore say to them, 'This is what the Sovereign LORD says: since you eat meat with the blood still in it and look to your idols and shed blood, should you then possess the land? You rely on your sword, you do detestable things, and each of you defiles his neighbour's wife. Should you then possess the land?'
> (Ezekiel 33:23–26)

The short answer is 'no'. God warns that they will be exiled from the land because of their arrogance and disobedience.

It is also hard to believe that the Jewish exiles in Babylon would have found Ezekiel's prophecy about the 'dry bones' much comfort, had he told them it wasn't actually for them but for their descendants living in the twentieth century. This kind of thinking that places our own generation at the centre of God's purposes isn't new. Intentionally or otherwise, this 'chronological arrogance' relegates previous generations to a kind of 'warm-up' act or prelude to the main event which is now. In the following few verses Ezekiel leaves us in no doubt as to the consequences of disobedience:

> 'I will make the land a desolate waste, and her proud strength will come to an end, and the mountains of Israel will become desolate so that no-one will cross them. Then they will know that I am the LORD, when I have made the land a desolate waste because of all the detestable things they have done.'
> (Ezekiel 33:28–29)

On the basis of such sober warnings it could be suggested that unless there is an imminent spiritual revival, Israel is more likely to experience another exile rather than a restoration. The Abrahamic and Mosaic promises were always conditional. 'Obey and stay, or rebel

and be removed.' The message of the prophets was consistent with
the warnings of the Torah. 'Repent and then return', never the other
way round.

The kingdom: nationalistic or universal?

While the boundaries of the land given to Abraham in Genesis 15 are
clear, the question remains as to whom they were intended for. Even
while the Israelites were wandering through the Sinai Desert, the Lord
indicated through Moses that he had given a portion of the land to the
children of Esau.

> For a long time we made our way around the hill country of Seir. Then
> the LORD said to me, 'You have made your way around this hill country
> long enough; now turn north. Give the people these orders: "You are
> about to pass through the territory of your brothers the descendants of
> Esau, who live in Seir. They will be afraid of you, but be very careful.
> Do not provoke them to war, for I will not give you any of their land,
> not even enough to put your foot on. I have given Esau the hill country
> of Seir as his own." '
> (Deuteronomy 2:1–5)

The region of Seir is between Mount Horeb and Kadesh Barnea in the
Negev (Deuteronomy 1:1–2, 44–46). So the region south of Beersheva,
although within the boundaries of the land given to Abraham, was
now allocated to the Edomites. The Israelites were therefore pro-
hibited from entering or settling in this area of the Negev. Those who
insist on 'biblical borders' for Israel need reminding that the modern
State of Israel is in possession of forbidden territory. Furthermore,
the means by which they have colonized the Negev, through the
forced expulsion of the indigenous Bedouin, is in clear breach of this
passage. As the Israelites in their wanderings travelled north to the
region of Moab, south-east of the Dead Sea, God gave them further
instructions:

> Then the LORD said to me, 'Do not harass the Moabites or provoke
> them to war, for I will not give you any part of their land. I have given
> Ar to the descendants of Lot as a possession ... When you come to the
> Ammonites, do not harass them or provoke them to war, for I will not

give you possession of any land belonging to the Ammonites. I have
given it as a possession to the descendants of Lot.'

(Deuteronomy 2:9, 19)

This vast region was also 'off-limits' to the Israelites because God had
allocated it to the descendants of Lot, the Moabites and Ammonites.
Today, Amman, the capital of Jordan, is named after their ancestors.

The kingdom of Israel reached its zenith in terms of extent, wealth,
power and influence in the ancient world under King David and King
Solomon (2 Samuel 8:1–14; 1 Kings 10:1–29). However, we learn
that Solomon gave away cities in Galilee to the Phoenicians. He traded
the towns in the Acre Valley as far as Rosh Hanikra, just south of Tyre
in Lebanon, in return for produce he needed for the construction of
the temple and his palaces in Jerusalem (1 Kings 9:11–13).

Ignoring the fact that Hiram wasn't particularly impressed with
them, it is significant that there were no prohibitions in the Mosaic
Law on the giving away of territory to non-Jews. What appears to
have mattered more were the strategic and economic interests of the
people, rather than the land itself being sacrosanct.

All was lost, however, when the kingdom was divided (1 Kings
11:31–39) and then first, in 722 BC, the northern tribes were taken
captive to Assyria (2 Kings 17) and then, beginning in 605 BC, the
remnant of Judah were exiled to Babylon (2 Kings 25). During this
time, God inspired Jeremiah to write a letter to the exiles, in which
he instructed them to settle down in Babylon and make it their
home. Indeed, they are told to work and pray for Babylon's peace
and prosperity (Jeremiah 29:4–7). Then he promised, after seventy
years, 'I will bring my people Israel and Judah back from captivity
and restore them to the land I gave to their ancestors to possess'
(Jeremiah 30:3).

The return of the exiles under Ezra and Nehemiah, while demon-
strating God's faithfulness, never matched the glory of the kingdom
under David or Solomon (Ezra 9:8–15; Nehemiah 9:28–37). And yet,
while the second exodus may have been more subdued, Jeremiah
describes it as far more significant than the first.

'So then, the days are coming,' declares the LORD, 'when people will no
longer say, "As surely as the LORD lives, who brought the Israelites up

out of Egypt," but they will say, "As surely as the LORD lives, who brought the descendants of Israel up out of the land of the north and out of all the countries where he had banished them." Then they will live in their own land.'
(Jeremiah 23:7–8)

Probably the greatest contrast between the two, however, concerns how the people already living in the land were to be treated. These are the instructions God gave to the returning exiles:

'You are to distribute this land among yourselves according to the tribes of Israel. You are to allot it as an inheritance for yourselves and for the foreigners residing among you and who have children. You are to consider them as native-born Israelites; along with you they are to be allotted an inheritance among the tribes of Israel. In whatever tribe foreigners reside, there you are to give them their inheritance,' declares the Sovereign LORD.
(Ezekiel 47:21–23)

So in the second exodus the Israelites are commanded to share the land with the 'foreigners' and treat them as equals – as 'native-born' Israelites. This return was to be peaceful and conciliatory. Although radical, this was entirely consistent with the instructions given in the law (Leviticus 19:33–34; see also Isaiah 56:3–8). The Promised Land under the old covenant was to be shared and inclusive. This is the biblical model many Christian Palestinians, who favour a one-state solution, long to see accepted within the modern State of Israel.

The Promised Land in the new covenant

Under Persian, then Greek and finally Roman occupation, the Jewish people longed for a Messiah to liberate them from the humiliation of foreign domination (Luke 1:68–79; John 6:14–15). This is probably why, after the resurrection of Jesus but before they came to recognize him, the disciples lamented his failure to restore political sovereignty to the Jews. This is reflected in their conversation on the road to Emmaus: 'we had hoped that he was the one who was going to redeem Israel' (Luke 24:21).

Is Jesus going to restore the kingdom to Israel?

After recognizing him as Lord and King, they then ask, 'Lord, are you at this time going to restore the kingdom to Israel?' (Acts 1:6). It is interesting that in this question the apostles at least see 'Israel' as having a separate existence as a people without sovereignty in the land. In his commentary, John Calvin writes, 'There are as many mistakes in this question as there are words.'[14] John Stott, in his commentary on the Acts of the Apostles, succinctly appraises errors made:

> The mistake they made was to misunderstand both the nature of the kingdom and the relation between the kingdom and the Spirit. Their question must have filled Jesus with dismay. Were they still so lacking in perception? ... The verb, the noun and the adverb of their sentence all betray doctrinal confusion about the kingdom. For the verb *restore* shows they were expecting a political and territorial kingdom; the noun *Israel* that they were expecting a national kingdom; and the adverbial clause *at this time* that they were expecting its immediate establishment. In his reply (7–8) Jesus corrected their mistaken notions of the kingdom's nature, extent and arrival.[15]

Since the Holy Spirit had not been given, the disciples may be forgiven for still holding to an old covenant understanding of the kingdom with the re-establishment of the monarchy and liberation from the brutal colonialism of Rome. Had they been present at Jesus' trial they might have understood things differently. Jesus explained, 'My kingdom is not of this world. If it were, my servants would fight to prevent my arrest by the Jews. But now my kingdom is from another place' (John 18:36).

Jesus repudiated the notion of an earthly and nationalistic kingdom on more than one occasion (see John 6:15). This is why, in reply to the disciples, Jesus says that he has another agenda for the apostles:

> It is not for you to know the times or dates the Father has set by his own authority. But you will receive power when the Holy Spirit comes on you; and you will be my witnesses in Jerusalem, and in all Judea and Samaria, and to the ends of the earth.
> (Acts 1:7–8)

The kingdom that Jesus inaugurated would, in contrast to their narrow expectations, be spiritual in character, international in membership and gradual in expansion. And the expansion of this kingdom throughout the world would specifically require their exile from the land. They must turn their backs on Jerusalem and their hopes of ruling there with Jesus in order to fulfil their new role as ambassadors of his kingdom (Matthew 20:20–28; 2 Corinthians 5:20–21). The Acts of the Apostles suggests that they needed something of a kick-start to get going. It is only when the Christians in Jerusalem experience persecution following the death of Stephen and are scattered, that they begin to proclaim the gospel to others (see Acts 8:1–4). The church was sent out into the world to make disciples of all nations but never told to return. Instead Jesus promises to be with them wherever they are in the world (Matthew 28:18–20).

The fig tree and David's fallen tent

Those who believe the New Testament speaks of a third Jewish return to the land quote the illustration of the fig tree in Matthew 24 and 'David's fallen tent' in Acts 15:13–17. Let's look at each briefly.

> Now learn this lesson from the fig-tree: as soon as its twigs become tender and its leaves come out, you know that summer is near. Even so, when you see all these things, you know that it is near, right at the door. I tell you the truth, this generation will certainly not pass away until all these things have happened.
> (Matthew 24:32–34)

The followers of Jesus understood him to be warning them to heed the signs and flee Jerusalem when the city came under Roman siege. Hal Lindsey, however, reverses its meaning. He claims Jesus was predicting the restoration of the Jews to Palestine in the twentieth century rather than their departure in the first century. How does he justify that?

> But the most important sign in Matthew has to be the restoration of the Jews to the land in the rebirth of Israel. Even the figure of speech 'fig tree' has been a historic symbol of national Israel. When the Jewish people, after nearly 2,000 years of exile, under relentless persecution, became a nation again on 14 May 1948 the 'fig tree' put forth its first leaves.[16]

You may need to read that again slowly. Do you see it? I don't either. It's called 'clutching at straws', or maybe in this case 'figs': reading back into a passage a subjective interpretation based on hindsight rather than foresight. Nothing in Matthew 24 leads us to believe Jesus wanted his hearers to understand that he was promising Israel would become a nation state once again. As we have already seen, Jesus has used the analogy of the fruit tree before: 'Therefore I tell you that the kingdom of God will be taken away from you and given to a people who will produce its fruit' (Matthew 21:43). Indeed, Jesus says that the subjects of the kingdom, that is, unbelieving Jews, will be 'thrown outside' (Matthew 8:10–12); none of those who were originally invited 'will get a taste of my banquet' (Luke 14:15–24). Nevertheless, Lindsey has popularized the notion that the return of Jewish people to Palestine since 1948 is somehow the fulfilment of biblical prophecy. Where did he get the idea from? Probably Cyrus Scofield.

Referring to Acts 15, Scofield asserts, 'dispensationally, this is the most important passage in the NT', since he claims, 'It gives the divine purpose for this age, and for the beginning of the next.'[17]

Here is the passage in question:

'After this I will return
  and rebuild David's fallen tent.
Its ruins I will rebuild,
  and I will restore it,
that the rest of humanity may seek the Lord,
  even all the Gentiles who bear my name,
says the Lord, who does these things' –
  things known from long ago.
(Acts 15:16–18)

James is simply quoting from Amos to show that Pentecost was not an accident, but had been predicted long ago. Amos foresaw how David's royal dynasty would be restored after the exile through one of his descendants – Jesus – and that through his victory on the cross and his reign over the nations, the Gentiles would also seek to enter his kingdom along with a Jewish remnant. Scofield, however, reads into this passage what is not there, while at the same time he obscures what is there. It all has to do with that little phrase 'after this'. The natural meaning is clear. James has in mind 'after the cross' or 'after the ascension' or even 'after Pentecost'. Scofield, however, claims once again, 'after this' means after another 2,000 years! He argues that God will one day soon 're-establish the Davidic rule over Israel'[18] and bring the Jewish people back to the land so that Jesus can rule as their king in Jerusalem.

The fact is that nowhere is a third re-gathering to the land explicitly mentioned in the Bible. The passages quoted by Scofield or Lindsey refer either to the first or second re-gathering to the land, or as in Amos 9, to Pentecost. It is significant that, following the rebuilding of the temple in 516 BC, there are no further biblical references to yet another return to the land, but plenty about exile from it.

Redefining the kingdom: an inclusive inheritance in the world

The New Testament knows nothing of this preoccupation with an earthly kingdom. As John Stott says, 'Christ's kingdom, while not incompatible with patriotism, tolerates no narrow nationalisms.'[19] Instead, Jesus redefines the boundaries of the kingdom of God to embrace the whole world. For example, in the Sermon on the Mount, Jesus takes a promise made to the Jewish people concerning the land from Psalm 37, and applies it to his own followers anywhere in the world (see Table 4.3).

Psalm 37:11	Matthew 5:5
But the meek will inherit the land and enjoy peace and prosperity.	Blessed are the meek, for they will inherit the earth.

Table 4.3.

Subsequent to Pentecost, under the illumination of the Holy Spirit, the apostles begin to use old covenant language concerning the land in new ways. Shortly after the day of Pentecost, Peter explains how the death, resurrection and ascension of Jesus had been predicted, inaugurating an expanded kingdom embracing all who would trust in Jesus.

Indeed, beginning with Samuel, all the prophets who have spoken have foretold these days. And you are heirs of the prophets and of the covenant God made with your fathers. He said to Abraham, 'Through your offspring all peoples on earth will be blessed.'

(Acts 3:24–25)

Here Peter claims that the promise made to Abraham (Genesis 12:3; 22:18) and repeated to Isaac (Genesis 26:4) and to Jacob (Genesis 28:14) was being fulfilled in the birth of the international community of Christ's followers.

In his letter to Christians dispersed throughout the Roman Empire, Peter writes in terms evoking memories of Abraham's journeying (Genesis 23:4), David's prayer (1 Chronicles 29:15), and the Jewish exiles in Babylon (Psalm 137:4). They are, he says, 'God's elect, exiles, scattered...' (1 Peter 1:1). He assures them, nevertheless, that their inheritance, unlike the land, '...can never perish, spoil or fade' (1 Peter 1:4).

Paul similarly asserts to the Christians in Galatia, 'If you belong to Christ, then you are Abraham's seed, and heirs according to the promise' (Galatians 3:29). In his letter to the church in Ephesus, he specifically applies the fifth commandment as promising an inheritance to Christian children (see Table 4.4).

Deuteronomy 5:16	Ephesians 6:1–3
Honour your father and your mother, as the LORD your God has commanded you, so that you may live long and that it may go well with you in the land the LORD your God is giving you.	Children, obey your parents in the Lord, for this is right. 'Honour your father and mother' – which is the first commandment with a promise – 'that it may go well with you and that you may enjoy long life on the earth.'

Table 4.4.

Children who willingly submit to the authority of their parents will, Paul promises, enjoy long life wherever they live on the earth.

When Paul meets the elders of the church in Ephesus on the beach at Miletus, he assures them a share in the same inheritance. 'Now I commit you to God and to the word of his grace, which can build you up and give you an inheritance among all those who are sanctified' (Acts 20:32).

The kingdom revealed in the mystery of Christ

But what of the hopes of the Jewish people in the new covenant? Paul visualized a more glorious future for the Jewish people – but not back in their land, rather in a covenant relationship with their Messiah, the Lord Jesus Christ (Romans 9 – 11).

In Romans 9, where Paul emphasizes how the Lord has not forgotten the Jewish people and that their hardening toward the gospel is only temporary, he lists the blessings they have received.

> I have great sorrow and unceasing anguish in my heart. For I could
> wish that I myself were cursed and cut off from Christ for the sake
> of my people, those of my own race, the people of Israel. Theirs is the
> adoption; theirs the divine glory, the covenants, the receiving of the
> law, the temple worship and the promises. Theirs are the patriarchs,
> and from them is traced the human ancestry of the Messiah, who is
> God over all, for ever praised! Amen.
> (Romans 9:2–5)

Significantly, Paul omits only one blessing, the land. There is no suggestion in Romans that the future salvation of the Jews is related in any way to the land. Instead Paul has already said, 'It was not through the law that Abraham and his offspring received the promise that he would be heir of the world, but through the righteousness that comes by faith' (Romans 4:13). The children of Abraham are those Jews and Gentiles who through faith in Christ have been made righteous. Together they have been made 'heirs of God and co-heirs with Christ' (Romans 8:17).

In his letter to the Ephesians, Paul explains that this progressive revelation of the will of God had been a mystery hidden until Jesus appeared.

> In reading this, then, you will be able to understand my insight into the
> mystery of Christ, which was not made known to people in other

generations as it has now been revealed by the Spirit to God's holy apostles and prophets. This mystery is that through the gospel the Gentiles are heirs together with Israel, members together of one body, and sharers together in the promise in Christ Jesus.
(Ephesians. 3:4–6)

The kingdom which Jesus heralded is therefore now internal not territorial. It is universal not tribal. When the Pharisees asked Jesus when the kingdom of God would appear, he replied, 'The coming of the kingdom of God is not something that can be observed, nor will people say, "Here it is," or "There it is," because the kingdom of God is within you.' (Luke 17:20–21). Jesus shatters the exclusive geographic straitjacket of the Pharisees and liberates the meaning of the covenant made with Abraham.

The inheritance of the saints was ultimately never an 'everlasting' share of the territory in Palestine but an eternal place in heaven. Indeed, the book of Hebrews shows that even Abraham, the Patriarchs and later Hebrew saints looked beyond Canaan to 'another' country in which the covenant promises of God would be fulfilled (Hebrews 11:10–16).

There is no evidence that the apostles believed that their inheritance was in Palestine, still less that the Jewish people had a divine right to the land in perpetuity, or that Jewish possession of the land would be an important, let alone central, aspect of God's purposes for the world.

The land had served its purpose, like an airport runway, to provide a temporary residence for the ancestors of the Messiah, David's greater Son; to host the incarnation, a home for the Lord Jesus Christ; and so be made for ever holy through the shedding of his innocent blood upon it. The land provided a base, a strategic launch pad for God's rescue mission, from which the apostles would take the good news of Jesus Christ to the world. In the New Testament, the land, like an old wineskin, had served its purpose. It was, and remains, irrelevant to God's ongoing redemptive purposes for the world.

Chapter summary points

- The covenant promises made to the Patriarchs concerning the land were understood as having been fulfilled in the Old Testament.
- The land, like the earth itself, belongs to God, and his people were at best foreigners and tenants with temporary residence.
- Residence in the land was always conditional and inclusive.
- Jesus repudiated a narrow nationalistic kingdom.
- His kingdom is spiritual, heavenly and eternal.
- This is the inheritance of all who trust in Jesus Christ.

Passages to review

Genesis 17:1–8; Deuteronomy 2:1–9; 28:1–10, 15–16, 63–64; Psalm 105:6–11, 37–45; Romans 9; Ephesians 3:4–6; Hebrews 11:10–16.

Questions for further study

1. Who was the Holy Land promised to and why?
2. What requirements were given for residency?
3. What significance does the Holy Land have in the New Testament?
4. What is the Christian's inheritance?

5. Battle for Jerusalem: The eternal capital of the Jews?

Many evangelicals, especially in America, accept unthinkingly the Zionist mantra that Jerusalem is the undivided, eternal and exclusive capital of the State of Israel. Today, Jerusalem lies at the heart of three world faiths – Judaism, Islam and Christianity. Israelis regard it as their capital. Palestinians do so also. Attempts to reach agreement in the wider Arab–Israeli conflict have stumbled partly over the contested status of Jerusalem. Jewish Zionists and their Christian supporters are strongly opposed to joint sovereignty or the recognition of East Jerusalem as the capital of Palestine. It seems time is on their side. The annexation of the Old City, the aggressive and illegal settlement programme, the systematic demolition of so many Arab homes and the construction of the Separation Barrier have all created 'facts on the ground' in Jerusalem. Christian and Jewish Zionists also claim a higher mandate for this agenda – the Word of God.

In this chapter we will consider why Jerusalem is so important to Christian Zionists and why they feel that only Jerusalem can be the exclusive capital of Israel. Then we will examine the place of Jerusalem in the Old Testament, and in particular some of the prophecies of Isaiah and Zechariah. We will go on to see what Jesus and the apostles have to say about the place of Jerusalem in the new covenant and especially in the end times.

The passion for Jerusalem

Following the Arab–Israeli war of 1967, Billy Graham's father-in-law, Nelson Bell, reflected the sentiments of many American Christians when he wrote, 'That for the first time in more than 2,000 years Jerusalem is now completely in the hands of the Jews gives a student of the Bible a thrill and a renewed faith in the accuracy and validity of the Bible.'[1]

Four years after the capture of Jerusalem, in June 1971, Carl Henry, then editor of *Christianity Today*, and considered the 'Dean' of American evangelical theologians, hosted a gathering in Jerusalem of over 1,200 evangelical leaders from thirty-two different countries. Welcomed by David Ben Gurion, the conference was billed as 'the first conference of its kind since A.D. 59'. Speakers, including W. A. Criswell, Harold Ockenga and John Walvoord, celebrated 'the regathering of Israel from the ends of the earth' and the capture of Jerusalem. These events were seen as 'confirmation that Jews and Israel still had a role to play in God's ordering of history' and that the return of Jesus was imminent.[2]

The wider international community saw things rather differently. In protest at Israel's unilateral annexation of East Jerusalem and the West Bank, the United Nations passed Resolution 242, calling on Israel to withdraw its troops to the June 1967 borders and end the occupation. Refusing to recognize Jerusalem as the capital of Israel, the few remaining government embassies were closed and relocated to Tel Aviv. In 1980, the International Christian Embassy (ICEJ) was founded in Jerusalem, to express solidarity with Israel and to recognize a divine blessing in the 'reunification' of Jerusalem under Israeli sovereignty. At the International Christian Zionist Congress in 1996, some 1,500 participants signed the following declaration.

> Because of the sovereign purposes of God for the City, Jerusalem must remain undivided, under Israeli sovereignty, open to all peoples, the capital of Israel only, and all nations should so concur and place their embassies here ... the truths of God are sovereign and it is written that the Land which He promised to His People is not to be partitioned.[3]

In 1997 the ICEJ also gave support to a full-page advert placed in the *New York Times* entitled, 'Christians Call for a United Jerusalem'. It was signed by ten evangelical leaders, including Pat Robertson, chairman of Christian Broadcasting Network and President of the Christian Coalition; Oral Roberts, founder and chancellor of Oral Roberts University; Jerry Falwell, founder of Moral Majority; Ed McAteer, President of the Religious Roundtable; and David Allen Lewis, President of Christians United for Israel:

> We, the undersigned Christian spiritual leaders, communicating weekly to more than 100 million Christian Americans, are proud to join together in supporting the continued sovereignty of the State of Israel over the holy city of Jerusalem. We support Israel's efforts to reach reconciliation with its Arab neighbors, but we believe that Jerusalem, or any portion of it, shall not be negotiable in the peace process. Jerusalem must remain undivided as the eternal capital of the Jewish people.[4]

They called upon fellow Christians to 'Join us in our holy mission to ensure that Jerusalem will remain the undivided, eternal capital of Israel.' 'The battle for Jerusalem has begun, and it is time for believers in Christ to support our Jewish brethren and the State of Israel. The time for unity with the Jewish people is now.'[5] They believed this would be achieved by the implementation of the Jerusalem Embassy Act, which legislates for the return of the US embassy back to Jerusalem. Funds have already been allocated. However, for more than ten years, successive US Presidents have vetoed the legislation for reasons of national security. Mike Evans, an outspoken critic, argues,

> Each time the national security waver is signed, we are saying to terrorists and bigots, 'You win.' America needs the blessings of God more than the favour with Arab bigots. Mr. Bush needs to send a signal to all the would-be Osamas that the party is over. No longer will America allow terrorists to threaten our nation into choosing political expediency over moral clarity.[6]

John Hagee, pastor of a mega-church in San Antonio, Texas, says that the special status afforded the Jewish people by God supersedes the rule of international law:

A shared Jerusalem? Never! A 'shared Jerusalem' means control of the
Holy City would be wrested away from the Jewish people and given,
at least in part, to the Palestine Liberation Organisation. I say 'never' . . .
because the Word of God says it is God's will for Jerusalem to be under
the exclusive control of the Jewish people until Messiah comes . . . God
doesn't care what the United Nations thinks . . . He gave Jerusalem to
the nation of Israel, and it is theirs.[7]

In 2003, the Jerusalem Summit, sponsored by the Unity Coalition
for Israel, issued their 'Jerusalem Declaration', in which they called
upon the international community to recognize:

> Billions of people believe that Jerusalem's spiritual and historical
> importance endows it with a special authority to become a center of
> world's unity.
>
> Israel's unique geographic and historic position at the crossroads of
> civilizations enables it to reconcile their conflicts. Israel's unique
> spiritual experience enables it to find a golden mean between the fault
> lines dividing civilizations: between tradition and modernity, religion
> and science, authority and democracy.
>
> We call upon all nations to choose Jerusalem, the eternal and
> indivisible capital of Israel, as a center for this evolving new unity.
> We believe that one of the objectives of Israel's divinely-inspired
> rebirth is to make it the center of the new unity of the nations,
> which will lead to an era of peace and prosperity, foretold by the
> Prophets.[8]

So they want Jerusalem to be a place of unity for the world, but not for
the people who live there! If this is representative of how pro-Zionist
Christians view Jerusalem, perhaps it is time we looked at what the
Scriptures have to say.

Jerusalem in the Old Testament

The story of Jerusalem goes way back as far as Genesis. It is possible
that Jerusalem was the home of Melchizedek, the priest and king who
blessed Abraham in Genesis 14. He is referred to as the 'king of Salem',
which later became identified in Jewish tradition with Jerusalem.
Mount Moriah, where Abraham offered Isaac as a sacrifice, is also later

identified in 2 Chronicles 3 as the same place where Solomon built his temple. Clearly, Jerusalem had an existence long before the conquest of the land by the Israelites. In Joshua 15:63, for example, we find the Jebusites already living in Jerusalem and willing to share the city with the new Jewish immigrants. It is clear, therefore, that Jerusalem was a shared city long before King David turned it into his capital (2 Samuel 6:1–19). Even then, the capture was achieved with minimal casualties on either side. It is also just possible that Zadok, David's high priest, was a Jebusite (1 Kings 2:35; 1 Chronicles 29:22) – Zedek was the Jebusite god of justice. So when Israel celebrated the 'Trimillennium of Jerusalem, City of David' in 1996, under the banner 'Jerusalem 3000', there was some legitimacy to the counter-claim launched by the Palestinian Authority to 'Jerusalem 5000'!

Clearly the building of the temple in Jerusalem by David's son, Solomon, elevated the status of the city among the tribes of Israel. However, when God judged Solomon for his idolatry (1 Kings 11:9–13), and his empire was split in two by Rehoboam and Jeroboam, Jerusalem diminished in importance and became just the capital for the tribe of Judah. As Peter Walker admits, 'The city designed to bring unity now pointed instead to Israel's division.'[9] Nevertheless, the belief grew that Jerusalem was invincible, because God dwelt in the temple and his anointed king was on the throne. Prophets such as Micah (3:9–12) and Jeremiah (7:1–11) warned against this arrogance. Jeremiah highlights one of the popular proverbs of the day. 'Do not trust in deceptive words and say, "This is the temple of the LORD, the temple of the LORD, the temple of the LORD!" ' (Jeremiah 7:4). Indeed, the prophet predicted that, far from defending Jerusalem in a 'holy war', God would actually become her enemy (Jeremiah 21:3–10).

The prophecies against Jerusalem came true in the capture and destruction of the city by the Babylonians under Nebuchadnezzar in 587 BC. The catastrophic events and the consequent exile of the Jews are recorded in 2 Kings 25, Jeremiah 52 and Lamentations. The prophetic message is clear. God holds his people morally accountable and will tolerate neither arrogance nor complacency.

Authors such as Hal Lindsey tend to ignore or minimize these warnings, preferring instead to focus on passages that speak of the significance of Jerusalem:

Jerusalem's importance in history is infinitely beyond its size and economic significance. From ages past, Jerusalem has been the most important city on this planet ... More prophecies have been made concerning Jerusalem than any other place on earth.[10]

One of these prophecies is found in Zechariah 14. It is frequently cited as evidence that one day soon all the nations of the earth will come to worship God in a newly built temple in Jerusalem. This is what Zechariah predicts:

> I will gather all the nations to Jerusalem to fight against it; the city will be captured, the houses ransacked, and the women ravished. Half of the city will go into exile, but the rest of the people will not be taken from the city ... Then the survivors from all the nations that have attacked Jerusalem will go up year after year to worship the King, the LORD Almighty, and to celebrate the Festival of Tabernacles.
> (Zechariah 14:2, 16)

Lindsey believes this prophecy is speaking about today and an imminent siege of Jerusalem by the Soviet army, rather than what happened in AD 70:

> There couldn't be a more perfect modern-day description of what was predicted hundreds of years ago in Zechariah 12 – 14. There it tells us that the last war of the world will be started by a dispute over Jerusalem. We've got that dispute right now. As a matter of fact, the West helped guarantee the world a dispute over Jerusalem by forcing the Israelis into a pact with the Palestinians.[11]

It was probably Cyrus Scofield who first popularized the idea that the Russians will attack Jerusalem in fulfilment of this prophecy and, '... that destruction should fall at the climax of the last mad attempt to exterminate the remnant of Israel in Jerusalem'.[12] How much of Jerusalem will be left standing when Jesus returns is a matter of speculation, given Lindsey's terrifying description of the war of Armageddon (more on this in chapter 7).

The Bible also makes clear that Jerusalem – the focal point of the endtimes fighting – will be vanquished by Israel's enemies in the hours just before the Lord comes. In fact, it seems that the destruction of the holy city is the final straw that angers God and provokes Jesus' return.[13]

Lindsey nevertheless looks forward to a better day after Armageddon, when, during the millennium, 'Jerusalem will be the spiritual centre of the entire world ... all people of the earth will come annually to worship Jesus who will rule there.'[14]

Now before we get carried away with this colourful interpretation of Zechariah, let's look again at the text. And remember ultra-literalism is like a sword – it cuts both ways. Notice that the purpose for 'going up to Jerusalem' is to celebrate the Feast of Tabernacles – something the International Christian Embassy does every autumn in preparation, as they see it, for the fulfilment of this prophecy. However, if you know your Old Testament feasts, you will know that the Feast of Tabernacles involves offering a rather large number of animal sacrifices (see Numbers 29:12–40 for the sacrifices expected – bulls, rams and lambs – and lots of them). If this makes you feel a little nervous (and it should), check out verse 15 where Zechariah describes the mode of transportation that will be used – 'horses and mules, the camels and donkeys' (Zechariah 14:15). This perhaps gives us a clue that Zechariah is describing events rather closer to his own day, or using contemporary imagery to describe future events surrounding the return of Jesus, the details of which (like the animal sacrifices, military tactics and means of transport) we do not therefore need to take literally. They are intended to encourage readers to trust in God's Messiah, who will overthrow evil and establish God's rule on earth for ever. What Zechariah predicts – the heathen nations coming to worship the one true God – is further developed in the Psalms and Isaiah.

In Psalm 87 we have a beautiful picture of a shared Jerusalem, an international and inclusive city where residency rights are determined by God on the basis of faith not race.

He has founded his city on the holy mountain.
The LORD loves the gates of Zion
    more than all the other dwellings of Jacob.

Glorious things are said of you,
   city of God:
'I will record Rahab and Babylon
   among those who acknowledge me –
Philistia too, and Tyre, along with Cush –
   and will say, "This one was born in Zion." '
Indeed, of Zion it will be said,
   'This one and that one were born in her,
   and the Most High himself will establish her.'
The LORD will write in the register of the peoples:
   'This one was born in Zion.'
As they make music they will sing,
   'All my fountains are in you.'
(Psalm 87)

As Colin Chapman has observed, 'This is a message which must have challenged many nationalistic prejudices.'[15] And one might add – still does.

Isaiah's vision of Jerusalem is also an inclusive one. In Isaiah 2, for example, we learn that people of many different nations will come to Jerusalem and put their faith in God and walk in his ways. One of the glorious consequences of this is that Jerusalem will become associated with the end of war, with peace and reconciliation between the nations (Isaiah 2:3–5).

The glorious future of Jerusalem is therefore one that impacts and benefits the entire world. Isaiah's vision is of an inclusive and shared Jerusalem, in which not only the Jewish people, but the nations themselves, are blessed. Perhaps this is why, when Jesus rebuked the religious leaders for exploiting the international visitors to the temple, he quotes from Isaiah: 'For my house will be called a house of prayer for all nations' (Isaiah 56:7, cf. Matthew 21:13).

So, despite what some would have us believe, the Old Testament vision of Jerusalem in the future is of an international, shared, inclusive city of faith, hope and love.

Jerusalem in the New Testament

What does the New Testament add to this vision? Well, there is some good news and some bad news. First, the bad news. It may surprise you to learn that the New Testament is rather pessimistic about the fate of Jerusalem. Far from promising a prosperous future at the centre of a revived Jewish state or even a millennial kingdom, Jesus lamented the impending destruction of Jerusalem. Luke's Gospel provides us with several insights into the passion of Jesus for Jerusalem. In Luke 13, we find Jesus rebuking the leaders of Israel for not caring for the people in the way he does, and predicting that he must die there. Evoking the language of Jeremiah (Jeremiah 12:7; 22:5), Jesus similarly laments:

> Jerusalem, Jerusalem, you who kill the prophets and stone those sent to you, how often I have longed to gather your children together, as a hen gathers her chicks under her wings, and you were not willing. Look, your house is left to you desolate. I tell you, you will not see me again until you say, 'Blessed is he who comes in the name of the Lord.'
> (Luke 13:34–35)

Quoting Psalm 118:26, Jesus also draws attention perhaps to a psalm in which, a few verses earlier, there is an enigmatic reference to his Messianic role: 'The stone the builders rejected has become the cornerstone' (Psalm 118:22). In the preceding verses Jesus contrasts his motives with those of Herod and the leaders of Jerusalem. He displays the instincts of a protective mother concerned for the people of Jerusalem as if they were his very children. A little later, on Palm Sunday, Jesus expresses perhaps his strongest emotions toward the city and its fickle people:

> As he approached Jerusalem and saw the city, he wept over it and said, 'If you, even you, had only known on this day what would bring you peace – but now it is hidden from your eyes. The days will come on you when your enemies will build an embankment against you and encircle you and hem you in on every side. They will dash you to the ground, you and the children within your walls. They will not leave one stone on another, because you did not recognise the time of God's coming to you.'
> (Luke 19:41–44)

Again, Jesus is using the language of Isaiah and Ezekiel to warn of God's impending judgment (Isaiah 29:3; Ezekiel 4:2). Now if you were there and heard Jesus make that prediction, who would you imagine he had in mind? Who were the hated enemies? The Romans of course. With the benefit of hindsight, it's obvious that Jesus was warning the people about what was going to happen very soon, not events 2,000 years or more in the distant future. With the total destruction of Jerusalem in AD 70, stone by stone, the slaughter of tens of thousands of Jews and the exile of the remnant as slaves of Rome, Jesus' sad prediction came true, to the letter.

The times of the Gentiles

But what about Luke 21:24 you may be thinking? This is a favourite verse among Christian Zionists, because they believe it describes the events of June 1967 and justifies the subsequent occupation and annexation of the Old City and East Jerusalem by Israel. Here are the words of Jesus, in context.

> When you see Jerusalem being surrounded by armies, you will know that its desolation is near. Then let those who are in Judea flee to the mountains, let those in the city get out, and let those in the country not enter the city. For this is the time of punishment in fulfilment of all that has been written. How dreadful it will be in those days for pregnant women and nursing mothers! There will be great distress in the land and wrath against this people. They will fall by the sword and will be taken as prisoners to all the nations. Jerusalem will be trampled on by the Gentiles until the times of the Gentiles are fulfilled.
>
> There will be signs in the sun, moon and stars. On the earth, nations will be in anguish and perplexity at the roaring and tossing of the sea. People will faint from terror, apprehensive of what is coming on the world, for the heavenly bodies will be shaken. At that time they will see the Son of Man coming in a cloud with power and great glory. When these things begin to take place, stand up and lift up your heads, because your redemption is drawing near.
>
> (Luke 21:20–28)

Hal Lindsey and Mike Evans are just two of the many contemporary prophecy experts who believe this passage is referring to our generation. In 1994 Lindsey was claiming 'We are literally witnessing the end of the times of the Gentiles.'[16] A year later he was a little more specific.

'We are literally witnessing the last hours of the times of the Gentiles. God's focus is shifting back to his people Israel.'[17] Mike Evans goes further, suggesting the 'times of the Gentiles' are now over.

> Through the centuries this prophecy has stood as an immovable landmark by which we may gauge the often confusing events of Jewish history . . . Jesus' words, spoken so long ago, make the city's recapture by the Jews, the single most prophetic event in history . . . The time of the Gentiles is now past and there has been a changing of the guard. Men may argue and pontificate, but something irrevocable has happened: Jerusalem is no longer trodden down by non-Jews. History has turned a corner – even if few have noticed it.[18]

What Evans and others have done to this passage is yet another example of exegesis by contemporary events, that is – reading back into Scripture subsequent events in history. The various editions of the *Scofield Reference Bible* provide a good example of this tendency. Notice how the footnote to Luke 21:24 changes after 1967 and becomes rather more enigmatic (see Table 5.1).

	Scofield Reference Bible (1917)	*The New Scofield Study Bible* (1984)
Luke 21:24	The 'times of the Gentiles' began with the captivity of Judah under Nebuchadnezzar, since which time Jerusalem has been under Gentile overlordship.[19]	The 'times of the Gentiles' began with the captivity of Judah under Nebuchadnezzar. Since that time Jerusalem has been, as Christ said, 'trampled on by the Gentiles'.[20]

Table 5.1.

Frankly, even with the benefit of hindsight, this is a rather weak basis for believing the Bible predicts a future 'restoration' of Jewish sovereignty over Jerusalem. Revelation 11:2 says that the Gentile 'trampling' of Jerusalem would continue for only '42 months'. If we take this literally as meaning three and a half years, dating this event is somewhat problematic. Is it past, present or future? Perhaps it's not surprising that Scofield does not link this passage to Jesus' prophecy! It is far more likely, as the TNIV Study Bible suggests, that the 'times of the Gentiles' is 'a conventional symbol for a limited period of time of unrestrained wickedness'.[21] If you re-read the context of Luke 21:24 again, you will see that in the preceding verses and even in the first part of verse 24 Jesus is still referring to events that occurred in AD 70. In verses 25–27 Jesus specifies cataclysmic events that will be associated with his return. In verse 28 Jesus gives encouragement to his followers, referring to 'your redemption', not to any 'redemption' of unbelieving Jerusalem.[22] It is therefore perhaps far wiser to follow commentators such as Norval Geldenhuys, who suggests that the 'times of the Gentiles' will not be fulfilled 'until the end of this present world-order when Christ will come with divine majesty and power to establish His eternal kingdom on the new earth after the Final Judgement (cf. verses 25–33)'.[23] Colin Chapman suggests an even simpler interpretation – that the 'times of the Gentiles' just means 'the time allowed to the Romans'.[24] In this sense, Jesus' words are a warning against Jewish pride in their city as much as Gentile arrogance in their military power. Both will be humbled on the day of judgment. It is also significant that Jesus uses the word 'trampled' to describe the effect of Gentile control. It's a word God uses repeatedly to describe his judgment in one of Isaiah's prophecies.

> I have *trodden* the winepress alone;
>> from the nations no-one was with me.
> I *trampled* them in my anger
>> and *trod* them down in my wrath . . .
> It was for me the day of vengeance;
>> the year for me to redeem had come . . .
> I *trampled* the nations in my anger;
>> in my wrath I made them drunk
>> and poured their blood on the ground.
> (Isaiah 63:3–6, emphasis added)

If this is the context for Jesus' words, then we learn from Isaiah that even the most powerful of human tyrants and empires are subject to God's sovereign will, and in some mysterious way fulfil his purposes and judgments. Jesus' statement in Luke 21:24 was therefore not intended to fuel 'end-time' speculation, but rather to encourage sober reflection on how we should live in the light of God's sovereign rule and judgment. In his death and resurrection, Jesus has brought redemption and restoration to all Jews and Gentiles who trust and believe in him. As Peter Walker observes:

> As for the future of Jerusalem, the Apocalyptic Discourse revealed that at the End, the central focus would not be upon Jerusalem, but rather upon the Son of Man ... if there was any connection with Jerusalem, it consisted in the fact that the End would be modelled typologically upon Jerusalem's destruction. The 'restoration' was of Jesus, not of Jerusalem.[25]

The challenge the apostles faced was proclaiming this good news among the very people who had crucified Christ. Despite the brutal power of the Roman occupation, the Jewish religious leaders in Jerusalem continued to exert immense influence over the Jews living throughout the Roman world. This tension spilled over into the early church. In his letter to the Galatians, Paul criticizes the legalists who had come from Jerusalem and who were infecting the church in Galatia with their mixture of law and grace and emphasis on circumcision. It appears they placed an undue emphasis on the significance of Jerusalem in determining Christian orthodoxy. As we have already seen, Paul is not impressed, comparing Jerusalem with Hagar and slavery rather than Sarah and the freedom found in the gospel. Instead he pointed to another more important Jerusalem.

The Jerusalem above

> But the Jerusalem that is above is free, and she is our mother. For it is written:
>
> > 'Be glad, barren woman,
> >   you who never bore a child;
> > break forth and cry aloud,
> >   you who were never in labour;

because more are the children of the desolate woman
than of her who has a husband.'
(Galatians 4:26–27; Isaiah 54:1)

In Galatians 4:27 Paul is quoting from Isaiah 54:1, which refers to the earthly Jerusalem. But Paul now interprets this passage as referring to the new Jerusalem, the home of all who believe in Jesus Christ, and no longer associated with the capital of Israel.[26] J. C. De Young writes:

Gal. 4:21 ff. represents, perhaps, the sharpest polemic against Jerusalem in the New Testament ... Far from being pre-occupied with hopes for a glorification of the earthly Jerusalem, Paul's thought represents a most emphatic repudiation of any eschatological hopes concerning the earthly city.[27]

The apostle John reaches the same conclusion in the book of Revelation. Here, Jerusalem becomes 'figuratively called Sodom and Egypt, where also their Lord was crucified' (Revelation 11:8): the Jerusalem that crucified Jesus Christ at the Passover; rejected the signs and wonders of the Holy Spirit at Pentecost; repudiated the message of the apostles; executed Stephen and James; tried to assassinate Paul; and instigated 'a great persecution ... against the church' (Acts 8:1). Therefore it has now become associated with the immorality of Sodom and the oppression of Egypt. The status of Jerusalem has changed irrevocably. From now on, the earthly Jerusalem will be associated not with the Patriarchs or with David or with the temple of Solomon or Herod but with a simple wooden cross and an empty tomb. 'The coming of Jesus has been its undoing.'[28] And here at last is a hint of the 'good news' about Jerusalem in the New Testament.

The good news about Jerusalem has to do with all that Jesus accomplished there. Peter Walker observes:

It is Jesus himself ... who gives us the warrant to view Jerusalem in an entirely new light ... Jerusalem could never be the same again, now that Jesus had come ... Jesus, not Jerusalem, would now become the central 'place' within God's purposes, the place around which God's true people would be gathered.[29]

The heavenly Jerusalem

The focus of the New Testament shifts away from an earthly to a heavenly Jerusalem of which, by faith in Jesus, we are already citizens. So, in Hebrews, for example, Christ's followers are promised residency in the heavenly Jerusalem.

> But you have come to Mount Zion, to the city of the living God, the heavenly Jerusalem. You have come to thousands upon thousands of angels in joyful assembly, to the church of the firstborn, whose names are written in heaven.
> (Hebrews 12:22–23)

Access to heaven no longer has anything to do with earthly Jerusalem. Jesus began to reveal this change in his conversation with a woman of Samaria.

> 'Woman,' Jesus replied, 'believe me, a time is coming when you will worship the Father neither on this mountain nor in Jerusalem. You Samaritans worship what you do not know; we worship what we do know, for salvation is from the Jews. Yet a time is coming and has now come when the true worshippers will worship the Father in Spirit and truth, for they are the kind of worshippers the Father seeks.'
> (John 4:21–23)

The new Jerusalem

It is true that some verses of the Old Testament can be interpreted as suggesting Jerusalem would be an exclusive city, reserved for one race, the Jewish people. For example, Isaiah refers to Jerusalem as a 'holy city' in which 'The uncircumcised and defiled will not enter you again' (Isaiah 52:1). However, this is most likely a reference to foreign invaders. By contrast, the image of Jerusalem found in the New Testament is of a new inclusive city built by God, coming down from heaven – one in which there is no darkness, and where the gates are never shut, but open to people of all nations.

> I saw the Holy City, the new Jerusalem, coming down out of heaven from God, prepared as a bride beautifully dressed for her husband . . .
> I did not see a temple in the city, because the Lord God Almighty and

the Lamb are its temple. The city does not need the sun or the moon to shine on it, for the glory of God gives it light, and the Lamb is its lamp. The nations will walk by its light, and the kings of the earth will bring their splendour into it. On no day will its gates ever be shut, for there will be no night there. The glory and honour of the nations will be brought into it. Nothing impure will ever enter it, nor will anyone who does what is shameful or deceitful, but only those whose names are written in the Lamb's book of life.
(Revelation 21:2, 22–27)

In this one all-consuming vision, God's people now embrace all peoples, God's land encompasses all nations, and God's holy city has become the eternal dwelling place of all who remain faithful – the Bride of Christ, the wife of the Lamb (Revelation 21:9). And what of the temple? John writes, 'I did not see a temple in the city, because the Lord God Almighty and the Lamb are its temple' (Revelation 21:22). And yet it is here that the contradiction between the flow of New Testament revelation and the Zionist agenda is most sharply brought into focus. The expectation of a future Jewish temple is probably the most controversial issue uniting Jewish Zionists and their Christian friends – and the subject of our next chapter.

Chapter summary points

- Christian Zionists defend and justify Israel's annexation of Jerusalem, claiming it is the eternal, undivided and exclusive capital of the Jews.
- Jerusalem became the capital of Israel briefly under David and Solomon, before its decline following the disintegration of tribal alliances and their eventual exile.
- The Old Testament vision of Jerusalem enjoying God's blessing is of an international and inclusive city of faith, justice and holiness.
- Jerusalem in the New Testament is associated not with Israel, the Jews or the temple, but with Jesus Christ, his death and resurrection.
- The end of the 'times of the Gentiles', far from being a sign of Jewish national sovereignty, more likely points to the return of Jesus.
- The Jerusalem that rejected Jesus and his followers is associated with the immorality of Sodom and oppression of Egypt in the book of Revelation.
- Christians look instead to a heavenly Jerusalem as their spiritual home.

Passages to review

2 Samuel 6:1–19; Psalm 87; Isaiah 2:3–5; 63:3–6; Jeremiah 7:1–11; 21:3–10; Micah 3:9–12; Matthew 23:37–39; Luke 13:34–35; 19:41–44; 21:20–28; John 4:21–23; Galatians 4:21–31; Hebrews 12:18–29; Revelation 21:1–27.

Questions for further study

1. What role does Jerusalem fulfil in the purposes of God?
2. Why did the prophets criticize the people of Jerusalem?
3. How did the coming of Jesus redefine the role of Jerusalem?
4. Why did Jesus weep over Jerusalem?
5. How should we interpret the 'times of the Gentiles' in Luke 21:24?
6. What do we learn about the 'new Jerusalem' from Psalm 87, Isaiah 2 and Revelation 21?
7. How should we pray for the peace of Jerusalem today?

6. The coming last days temple: Ready to rebuild?

Just 500 metres by 300 metres, the Temple Mount, or Haram Al Sharif as it is called in Arabic, is probably the most disputed plot of land on earth. Hal Lindsey claims, 'I believe the fate of the world will be determined by an ancient feud over 35 acres of land.'[1]

Many Christians share the belief that the Islamic shrines must be destroyed and that a Jewish temple must and will be rebuilt – very soon. This temple won't be a museum replica of the one king Solomon built, nor will it be just another attraction for pilgrims to the Holy Land. It will be built for one purpose and one purpose only – for bloody animal sacrifices, and lots of them.

In this chapter we want to explore the case for rebuilding the Jewish temple, to consider whether the Bible predicts such an event, and if so, where and how it might be built. We will then look at what the New Testament has to say on the subject, and some of the implications for Christianity should the Jewish temple be rebuilt. Finally, we will reveal that the temple is actually under construction (but don't peep).

However eccentric or strange it may seem, influential Christian leaders are actively promoting and funding Jewish religious groups who want to destroy the Dome of the Rock in Jerusalem, the third most holy shrine within Islam. They want to replace it with a fully functioning Jewish temple. They are doing so because they believe the Bible mandates it. Indeed, some Christians such as pastor Clyde Lott, a Pentecostal rancher from Mississippi, are even trying to breed the perfect red heifer to assist in future temple sacrifices. According to the book of Numbers chapter 19, the ashes of a red heifer are needed to purify the priests and altar before sacrifices can be offered again.[2] The search for the red heifer has been described as a 'four-legged time bomb'.

Others, such as Christians United for Israel (CUFI), appear so embarrassed by the presence of the Islamic Dome of the Rock dominating the view of Jerusalem, that they simply airbrushed it out of their picture. The banner photo at the top of their website initially showed a photo of the Western Wall with the trees growing above on the Haram Al Sharif, but with no Dome of the Rock. No Al-Aqsa. They had vanished. Then, just as mysteriously, perhaps due to criticism, an image of the Dome of the Rock suddenly reappeared. The problem is, in their photo it is now relocated a few hundred metres to the north of where it should be, presumably making room for the new Jewish temple. The angles are just wrong since the El-Silsilah minaret has also now appeared almost in front of the Dome, suggesting another photo taken from the north has been super-imposed on one taken from the west. Maybe a picture of the Jewish temple will suddenly appear soon as well. As a colleague observed, 'It's there, but shouldn't be there ... in the hope it that one day it WON'T be there ...'

> The thousand words painted by this picture is an essay on fundamentalist Christian Zionist fantasies ... A fantasy world in which there are no Palestinians ... Even more frightening is the possibility that those who live with this illusion will take steps to make the fantasy come true – to destroy the two mosques which were absent in the CUFI photo.[4]

What makes their plans even more bizarre is that they believe the temple must be rebuilt just so that it can be desecrated one more time by the Antichrist before Jesus returns. They believe Daniel and Matthew predict the temple will be desecrated before Jesus returns to rescue Israel and defeat her enemies in the 'battle for Jerusalem'.[5]

Unfortunately, this is not just some wacky belief held by a small group of fanatics. In 1989, *Time* magazine reported the findings of a survey showing that some 18% of Israelis thought it was time to rebuild the temple.[6] By 1996, when the Temple Mount Faithful sponsored a Gallup poll seeking a referendum on replacing the Al-Aqsa Mosque with a Jewish temple, support for the action had risen to 58%.[7] When you realize that Arab Israelis, who are mostly Muslim, would certainly not back the idea, the percentage of Jewish Israelis who do so must be even higher. What makes this poll even more significant is that while Israeli society is divided on just about every other subject, according to the Gallup poll, this was the largest show of support any Israeli organization has ever received on any issue.[8]

It gets more ominous still. On 8 January 2001, former Shin Bet secret service chief Carmi Gillon and former police commissioner Assaf Hefetz, together with leading Israeli academics, delivered a report to the then Israeli Prime Minister Ehud Barak, detailing their concerns regarding plots by Jewish extremist groups to blow up the Dome of the Rock and Al-Aqsa Mosque. Keshev, the Centre for the Protection of Democracy, based in Tel Aviv, founded by Gillon and Hefetz following the assassination of Rabin, published a twelve-page report entitled 'Target Temple Mount', which examined current threats to the Temple Mount from extreme militant and Messianic groups. The report claimed, 'The Temple Mount is like a smouldering volcano that is bubbling and threatening to erupt – a threat that is liable to endanger Israel's existence.'[9] And the tragedy is that some Christians are ready to light the fuse. On the same day, around 500,000 secular, religious and ultra-Orthodox Jews gathered near the Temple Mount at the Western Wall 'and swore faithfulness to the Temple Mount and Jerusalem'.[10]

Six months later in July 2001, the Rabbinical Council of Judea, Samaria and Gaza called on all rabbis to bring their communities to visit the Temple Mount. This was the first time a group of rabbis representing a significant proportion of the religious Jewish community had ruled it permissible for Jews to ascend the Temple Mount. Previously this had been forbidden. The rabbis also called upon the Yesha Council of Jewish settlements to organize mass visits to the Temple Mount from the settlements.[11]

So what on earth would lead so many Jews and Christians to agree on such a provocative and dangerous plan that could very well start World

War 3? As scary as it may seem, they simply believe the Bible not only predicts but indeed requires them to help rebuild the Jewish temple, with no fear of the consequences. Let's consider their arguments.

The case for rebuilding the temple

Hal Lindsey is dogmatic: 'Obstacle or no obstacle, it is certain that the Temple will be rebuilt. Prophecy demands it ... It is like the key piece of a jigsaw puzzle being found ... it is a time of electrifying excitement.'[12] What prophecy 'demands it'? Well, the argument goes way back to Exodus where God instructed Moses, 'Then have them make a sanctuary for me, and I will dwell among them' (Exodus 25:8). Orthodox Jews clearly do not recognize Jesus as their Messiah, so they believe the instructions given in the Hebrew Scriptures still apply. Exodus 25 – 40, for example, explains how Moses was to construct the tabernacle, while Leviticus 1 – 7 outlines the various offerings God required from his people. Orthodox Jews believe that a temple is necessary for them to offer sacrifices once again to make atonement for their sin. This is why religious Jews pray three times every day that 'the Temple be speedily rebuilt in our days'. They claim the Torah, or Law of Moses, 'obligates the Jewish nation to rebuild the Temple whenever it becomes possible to do so (Ex 25:8)'.[13]

Some Messianic Jews (that is, Jewish believers in Jesus) are also sympathetic to the idea that a temple is necessary for Jews to atone for their sins. Visit the Jews for Jesus website and you can read an article by Zhava Glaser, where she asks rhetorically,

> Though some rabbis might minimize the revealed system of worship and its requirements, can the individual Jew neglect what God says? Can there be a 'proper' Judaism without a priesthood, an altar, a sacrifice and a place on earth where God meets the individual?[14]

The answer to Glaser is obviously 'no'. This is also the reason why some Christian Zionist organizations celebrate the Feast of Tabernacles in Jerusalem each year. They are anticipating the day when, according to their literal reading of Zechariah 14, they believe everyone, including you and me, will go to Jerusalem annually to worship God.[15]

However, in the vision of the temple found in Ezekiel 40 – 46, this instruction is given: 'you are to give a young bull as a sin offering'

(Ezekiel 43:19). For Christians who support the rebuilding of the temple, this verse must stick in the throat. To change the anatomical analogy, it is actually the 'Achilles' heel' of those who read the Bible in an ultra-literal way. Why? Because the verse requires the reintroduction of animal sacrifices. Cyrus Scofield, in his *Reference Bible*, fudges the issue, claiming these will only be 'memorial' offerings.[16] Schuyler English and the editorial committee of *The New Scofield Study Bible* dig a hole for themselves when they claim:

> The reference to sacrifices is not to be taken literally, in view of the putting away of such offerings, but is rather to be regarded as a presentation of the worship of redeemed Israel, in her own land and in the millennial Temple, using the terms with which the Jews were familiar in Ezekiel's day.[17]

Scofield was the great exponent of literalism. If we are to take the Bible literally, then the sacrifice of a 'young bullock' cannot be mistaken for a 'memorial offering' that consisted of grain and oil. The story of Cain and Abel reminds us of the hazards of offering God the wrong kind of sacrifice (Genesis 4:4–7)! If this particular reference to sacrifice in Ezekiel 43 need not be taken literally, then what is all the fuss about? Why is it necessary to take other Old Testament prophecies 'literally' and apply them to Israel today if not this one? Sounds a little inconsistent doesn't it? They want to have their cake and eat it – or in this case, they want their sacrifices without the blood.

The context for Ezekiel's vision of a rebuilt temple is actually the promised return of the Jews from Babylonian exile, not an event that might happen around 2,500 years later! It would have been utterly meaningless for the exiles longing to return to Israel to be told 'Be encouraged. Although this doesn't apply to you, it is going to happen in a few thousand years' time.'

The most frequently quoted passage in the Bible used to justify the rebuilding of the Jewish temple is Daniel 9:26–27. This is what the passage says:

> The people of the ruler who will come will destroy the city and the sanctuary ... war will continue until the end ... He will confirm a covenant with many for one 'seven'. In the middle of the 'seven' he

will put an end to sacrifice and offering. And at the temple he will set up an abomination that causes desolation, until the end that is decreed is poured out on him.

(Daniel 9:26–27)

Now, don't get hung up over the number 'seven'. Advocates assume 'seven' refers to a period of seven years. Let's concede this for the moment. What you need to focus on instead is the fact that in verse 26 Daniel says a powerful ruler will come and 'destroy the city and the sanctuary', and then in verse 27 'he will put an end to sacrifice' and 'set up an abomination'. Between the two you have a hint of a time scale: 'War will continue until the end.' Authors such as Hal Lindsey and David Brickner believe Daniel is speaking chronologically and that 'the end' literally means 'the end of the world'. Brickner puts it this way:

> Obviously the Temple has been rebuilt because Daniel tells us this ruler puts an end to sacrifice and sets up some kind of abomination (a loathsome horror that would be anathema to Jewish worship) right inside the Temple in Jerusalem. Ultimately this ruler is destroyed in a final conflagration of enormous proportion.[18]

Now you may need to make a strong coffee at this point and read the passage a few more times to understand the logic. Put simply, the question is: How can Daniel refer to sacrifices coming to an end in verse 27 when the temple has apparently already been destroyed in verse 26? Simple – Daniel must be talking about two different temples! So verse 26 must be describing what happened in AD 70 when the Romans destroyed Herod's temple, and verse 27 must refer to a future temple. To justify this interpretation, however, it is necessary to place a 2,000-year gap or 'parenthesis' between verses 26 and 27, and argue that the prophetic clock stopped during what is called the 'church age' or the 'times of the Gentiles' (Luke 21:24).

The fact that Hezekiah's temple was desecrated by Antiochus Epiphanes in 168 BC and then in AD 67–70 Herod's temple was desecrated, first by Jewish Zealots and then again by Titus and his Roman army during the Jewish Revolt, apparently doesn't count. It has got to happen all over again. The argument falls to the ground, however, if you don't believe Daniel's vision is describing two separate events separated by thousands of years.

The other favourite passage of temple watchers is Matthew 24:1–2, 15–16.

> Jesus left the temple and was walking away when his disciples came up to him to call his attention to its buildings. 'Do you see all these things?' he asked. 'I tell you the truth, not one stone here will be left on another; every one will be thrown down ... So when you see standing in the holy place "the abomination that causes desolation," spoken of through the prophet Daniel – let the reader understand – then let those who are in Judea flee to the mountains.
>
> (Matthew 24:1–2, 15–16)

In case you don't get the plot here either, in his book *Apocalypse Code*, Lindsey thoughtfully adds words to the biblical text to help you out. So Matthew 24:15 reads, 'So when you see standing in the holy place [of the rebuilt Temple] the abomination ... '[19]

To be consistent with their interpretation of Daniel, those advocating the need for another Jewish temple must again add a 2,000-year chasm between Jesus' words in verses 1–2 and verses 15–16. Frankly, I'd much rather accept the eyewitness account of the first-century Jewish historian, Flavius Josephus, who describes how Daniel's prophecy came true before his very eyes in AD 67–70.[20]

There is actually nothing in the text of Daniel, Matthew, or anywhere else in the Bible, that suggests or requires a 2,000-year gap between the verses of these two passages. To put it kindly, Lindsey and his colleagues are 'pulling a fast one' over the text of Scripture. Why? Your guess is as good as mine, although this kind of tabloid journalism linking the Bible with contemporary events is certainly the way to sell books, at least first editions. Hal Lindsey claims his book, *The Late Great Planet Earth*, at 15 million copies in over thirty languages, has 'sold more copies than any Christian book in history other than the Bible'.[21] Thankfully the Bible is easier to read, never goes out of date and is much more popular.

If the biblical case for rebuilding the temple is rather suspect, the quest for locating its original foundations reads more like something out of an *Indiana Jones* script.

The quest to build the 'last days' temple

Even though many Jews and Christians believe the temple must be rebuilt, there is one small problem. It is essential that any future temple is built on the same foundations as the previous ones. And on this rather fundamental point experts cannot agree. Where was the Holy of Holies located? The simple answer is 'we don't know'. While it may not particularly matter to any budding antichrists, it does matter to the ultra-Orthodox Jews. When Jesus predicted the Romans would not leave one stone left on another and that 'every one will be thrown down' (Matthew 24:2), he was right. The Romans fulfilled Jesus' prediction to the letter when they burned to the ground and then flattened Herod's temple along with the rest of Jerusalem. Two thousand years later, the quest to find the site of the temple is causing a good deal of heated debate within Israeli archaeological circles.

There are four contenders, each with their scholarly advocates and scientific theories. Unfortunately, the Dome of the Rock is situated over the most popular site. Inside the third most holy shrine to over one billion Muslims is a rocky outcrop on which Jews believe Abraham offered Isaac. Beneath it is a very ancient cave with a hole in the roof that looks remarkably like the place where the blood from the temple sacrifices might have been collected and flushed away. It is now a place of prayer for Muslims.

Lindsey must be living on another planet when he suggests a future Jewish temple could be built right alongside the Dome of the Rock. Somehow I don't think the Muslim authorities are going to agree to move it elsewhere or allow a Jewish temple to be built alongside it. But Lindsey claims it could revive the Israeli economy and become 'the greatest tourist attraction in the world'. He goes on to say, 'Right now, as you read this, preparations are being made to rebuild the Third Temple.'[22]

On the last point at least, Lindsey is right. Building a temple with all the fancy architectural detail stipulated by Ezekiel is going to be pretty expensive. So who is going to foot the bill? You guessed it – gullible Christians who believe they are helping speed the return of Jesus. I was in Colorado Springs recently when Gershon Salomon was also speaking – in his case at one of the largest churches in town, raising funds for his organization. Grace Halsell estimates that at least $100 million a year is being raised by some rather well-known televangelists and church leaders to rebuild the temple.[23] And if you want to know where to send your own donation, Randall Price in his book, *The Coming Last Days Temple*, provides you with the contact details of all the Jewish organizations committed to rebuilding the Jewish temple.[24]

Armageddon and the temple of doom

In the prologue to his book *Kingdoms in Conflict*, Charles Colson describes a very realistic scenario in which an American president (probably modelled on Ronald Reagan) is faced with the hardest decision of his life. Jewish terrorists have blown up the Dome of the Rock and are being filmed live on Christian TV channels. Raised as a Christian Zionist, the president believes the Bible predicts the rebuilding of the temple, but his military advisors urge him to send in the US marines to intervene, occupy the Temple Mount and maintain the status quo. What is he to do? Colson leaves you with the dilemma unresolved, but with the clock ticking. Although a fictional scenario, he assures us in a footnote that the US military have anticipated such an event and have plans in place if and when it happens.[25] That may or may not fill you with much confidence.

In fact, this is not just fictional speculation. While some Zionists are praying like crazy for an earthquake to do it for them, others like Gershon Salomon and his Temple Mount Faithful are unwilling to wait for divine intervention.

In July 2001, the Israeli Supreme Court made a significant decision. For the first time ever they allowed the Temple Mount Faithful to hold a symbolic cornerstone-laying ceremony for the third temple near the Dung Gate adjacent to the Western Wall. Every year since then, attempts have been made to carry their three-ton cornerstone onto the Temple Mount on Tisha B'Av (29 July). That is the day when the Jews mourn the destruction of the first and second temples. In 2006, despite police objections, the Israeli Supreme Court gave permission for members of the Temple Mount Faithful actually to enter the area of the Haram Al Sharif on the festival of Tisha B'Av. An Israeli Arab MP, Mohammed Barakeh, described the High Court's decision as 'petrol in the hands of declared pyromaniacs'. To pre-empt a massacre, the police closed the site to Jews as well as to Muslims for the whole day, based on intelligence reports that thousands of Muslims were planning to flock to the site to protect it.[26]

It seems that it is more a question of 'when' not 'whether' this will happen. Speaking at a Christian Zionist conference in Jerusalem recently, Gershon Salomon stated:

> The Israeli Government must do it. We must have a war. There will be many nations against us but God will be our general. I am sure this is a test, that God is expecting us to move the Dome with no fear from other nations. The Messiah will not come by himself, we should bring him by fighting.[27]

Shades of Judas and the first-century Zealots who tried to force the hand of God to act. It is sobering to learn that since 1967 there have been no less than 100 armed assaults on the Haram Al Sharif, often led by Jewish rabbis. That averages out to more than two a year. Sadly, the Israeli authorities, political and religious, have yet to condemn any of these attacks.[28]

Gordon Welty, an anthropologist, explains the apparent contradiction of evangelical Christians claiming to follow Jesus, yet choosing to support Jewish terrorists.

> Their power is to keep inconsistencies in airtight compartments, so that they themselves never recognize these inconsistencies ... If the money a muscular Christian donates to the Jewish terrorists buys the dynamite that destroys the mosque, the muscular Christian will say simply, 'It was an act of God'.[29]

As Lawrence Wright has observed, 'Jewish longing for the Temple, Christian hopes of the Rapture, and Muslim paranoia about the destruction of the mosques [are being] stirred to an apocalyptic boil.'[30] We wait with bated breath.

The temple: redundant before it is even built

The problem with all this speculation about a future temple in Jerusalem is simply this – from a Christian perspective, it is heresy. There is absolutely nothing in the New Testament about the need for another temple in Jerusalem: just the reverse – the old temple was declared redundant the moment Jesus died on the cross. The curtain separating the people from the Holy of Holies was torn in two –

significantly from top to bottom. That is why the writer to the Hebrews says: 'By calling this covenant "new", he has made the first one obsolete; and what is obsolete and outdated will soon disappear' (Hebrews 8:13). This is the theological explanation for the destruction of the temple in AD 70. It had served its purpose. The true temple had arrived.

In fact, it was never God's intention that a temple be built in the first place. Like Israel's desire for a king, it was more a sign that they wanted to be like the surrounding nations rather than wanting to do his will (see 1 Samuel 8:6–9). Having captured Jerusalem and built a palace for himself, David's impulse was to build a temple for God as well. When he asked Nathan the prophet for advice, this is the reply he received:

> Go and tell my servant David, 'This is what the LORD says: are you the one to build me a house to dwell in? I have not dwelt in a house from the day I brought the Israelites up out of Egypt to this day. I have been moving from place to place with a tent as my dwelling. Wherever I have moved with all the Israelites, did I ever say to any of their rulers whom I commanded to shepherd my people Israel, "Why have you not built me a house of cedar?" '
> (2 Samuel 7:5–7)

In a play on words, God then tells David he is not to build a house (temple) for God, but instead God will build a house (dynasty) for David. Just as God gave in to Israel's desire for a king, so he tells David that he will allow his son Solomon to build him a house, although the impression given is that God preferred to dwell with his people in a tabernacle, because it kept his people dependent on his leading.

The true and lasting temple is Jesus. The sanctuary in Jerusalem, however beautiful, was only ever a copy and shadow of the heavenly one (Hebrews 8:1–5). This is how Jesus introduces the idea in John 2.

> Jesus answered them, 'Destroy this temple, and I will raise it again in three days.' They [the Jews] replied, 'It has taken forty-six years to build this temple, and you are going to raise it in three days?' But the temple he had spoken of was his body.
> (John 2:19–21)

When Jesus entered the temple and threw out the money changers, he wasn't 'cleansing' it for future use. He was declaring it redundant. He himself is the one and only true temple. The temporary earthly replica was now close to its 'sell-by' date. The real, more glorious and lasting temple had arrived. That is why, in his conversation with the Samaritan woman, Jesus said we could now worship God anywhere (John 4:21–24).

Jesus warned his followers to escape from Jerusalem when they saw the Roman army beginning to surround the city. He predicted that Herod's temple, although unfinished, would be destroyed (Matthew 24:15–20). The only temple Jesus ever promised would be rebuilt was his body – in three days. Why? Because Jesus made the temple redundant. The writer of Hebrews says, 'After he finished the sacrifice for sins...' (Hebrews 1:3, *Message*). Jesus fulfilled the role of temple, high priest and sacrificial lamb. That is why the offering of sacrifices since the death of Christ is now utterly futile. Only Jesus can take away our sin. Hebrews goes on to explain:

> The law is only a shadow of the good things that are coming – not the realities themselves. For this reason it can never, by the same sacrifices repeated endlessly year after year, make perfect those who draw near to worship. Otherwise, would they not have stopped being offered? For the worshippers would have been cleansed once for all, and would no longer have felt guilty for their sins. But those sacrifices are an annual reminder of sins ... Day after day every priest stands and performs his religious duties; again and again he offers the same sacrifices, which can never take away sins.
> (Hebrews 10:1–3, 11)

The writer quotes from Psalm 40:6–8 to show that obedience is more important than sacrifice, and that the obedience of the Son of God in the offering of his body would supersede and annul the need for the perpetual offering of animal sacrifices.

> First he said, 'Sacrifices and offerings, burnt offerings and sin offerings you did not desire, nor were you pleased with them' – though they were offered in accordance with the law. Then he said,

'Here I am, I have come to do your will.' He sets aside the first
to establish the second. And by that will, we have been made
holy through the sacrifice of the body of Jesus Christ once
for all.

(Hebrews 10:8–10)

God used the Roman general Titus to destroy the temple in the same
way he had used the Babylonian King Cyrus to help build it. When
Jesus cried out 'It is finished' as he died on the cross, he did indeed
'make perfect those who draw near to worship ... [and] take away
sins' (Hebrews 10:1, 4).

The temple sacrifices, at best, only ever provided a temporary
cover for sin. The daily sacrifices, and the smoke rising from the altar,
were a constant reminder of the need for a Saviour. How then could
God encourage the sacrificial system to be reinstated when he had sent
his son Jesus to be the ultimate sacrifice, to shed his own blood on the
cross to take away our sin? To suggest sacrifices must be made once
more undermines the New Testament's teaching that the work of
Christ is sufficient, final and complete.

The true temple is already under construction
Those who advocate the need for a new temple and the reintroduction of sacrifices are ignoring the way the image of the
temple is invested with new meaning. Subsequent to Pentecost,
the temple imagery is applied to the church, the body of Christ, the
dwelling place of the Holy Spirit. For example, Paul, writing to
the church in Ephesus, describes them as part of the new living
temple.

Consequently, you are ... members of [God's] household, built on the
foundation of the apostles and prophets, with Christ Jesus himself as the
chief cornerstone. In him the whole building is joined together and rises
to become a holy temple in the Lord.

(Ephesians 2:19–21)

In his letter to the Corinthians, Paul quotes from passages in
Leviticus and Isaiah, both of which refer to the physical tabernacle and
temple, and applies them to the church.

For we are the temple of the living God. As God has said:

'I will live with them
  and walk among them,
and I will be their God,
  and they will be my people.'
Therefore,
'Come out from them
  and be separate,
                    says the Lord.
Touch no unclean thing,
  and I will receive you.'
(2 Corinthians 6:16–17, citing Leviticus 26:12 and Isaiah 52:11)

In his letter to the Romans, Paul uses temple language to describe how we are to offer, not a dead animal sacrifice, but our bodies as living sacrifices as our act of worship (Romans 12:1–2).

Similarly, Peter describes the church using Hebrew imagery associated with the temple (Psalm 118:22; Isaiah 28:16). Christians are, he says, being made into the new house for God, in which Jesus is the 'precious cornerstone' (1 Peter 2:5–7). So the temple in Jerusalem was intended to be only a temporary building, a shadow pointing to the day when God would dwell with people of all nations through Jesus Christ.

The flow of biblical revelation is progressive and moves in one historical direction. Christians who support the rebuilding of the temple in the belief that future sacrifices will be memorial offerings, or can even atone for sin, are committing apostasy. Why? Because they are trying to reverse the flow of revelation and go back to the shadows when we already have the light of Christ. In the words of the writer to the Hebrews:

It is impossible for those who have once been enlightened, who have tasted the heavenly gift, who have shared in the Holy Spirit, who have tasted the goodness of the word of God and the powers of the coming age and who have fallen away, to be brought back to repentance. To their loss they are crucifying the Son of God all over again and subjecting him to public disgrace.
(Hebrews 6:4–6)

And that is the final rub. People must choose between a religion and a relationship; between the words 'do' and 'done'; between law and grace; between the need to offer continual sacrifices for sin or accept the finished work of Jesus Christ in our place; between a physical temple and a spiritual one; between one in Jerusalem that is redundant and one that encompasses the whole world that is under construction.

In this chapter we have considered the case for rebuilding the Jewish temple. We have examined some of the biblical passages used to justify the construction of yet another temple in Jerusalem, and we have seen that there is in fact not a single verse in the entire New Testament which predicts that a Jewish temple will ever be rebuilt or that a 2,000-year 'parenthesis' should be placed between references to its desecration and destruction in Daniel, or that a future temple in Jerusalem will play any part in God's future purposes. We have also seen how the followers of Jesus Christ are a living temple, indwelt by the Holy Spirit.

How tragic that, while the good news of Jesus is intended to bring peace and reconciliation with God and healing between nations, some Christians are fuelling religious hatred, and are bent on inciting an apocalyptic war.

Chapter summary points

- Attempts by militant Jewish groups to destroy the Dome of the Rock and rebuild the Jewish temple have widespread support and are taken very seriously by the Israeli authorities.
- Any attempt to rebuild the temple will very likely ignite an apocalyptic war with Muslims worldwide.
- For some, the case for rebuilding the temple is based on the mistaken belief that only through the reintroduction of the sacrificial system can Jewish people atone for their sins.
- For others, the temple must be rebuilt so that it can be desecrated one more time before Jesus returns.
- This is only possible by the insertion of a 2,000-year gap between Daniel 9:26 and 9:27 and Matthew 24:1–2 and 24:15–16.
- This assumption must ignore the way in which previous temples were desecrated by Antiochus Epiphanes and the Jewish Zealots, as well as by Titus and the Roman army.
- There are four different possible locations for Herod's temple, therefore no consensus as to where any new Jewish temple might be built.
- There is not a single verse in the New Testament that requires or justifies a temple in Jerusalem.
- The temple was made redundant and obsolete when Jesus, the true temple, died on the cross.
- The church, the body of Christ, is likened to a living temple.
- The apostles apply Old Testament temple references to the church.
- To advocate the rebuilding of the temple is heresy.

Passages to review
2 Samuel 7:1–17; John 4:21–24; Hebrews 9 – 10; Ephesians 2:19–21; 1 Corinthians 6:19; 2 Corinthians 6:16; 1 Peter 2:9; Revelation 21:9–27.

Questions for further study

1. What role did the temple fulfil under the old covenant?
2. Why is an earthly temple no longer required?
3. What or who is the temple?
4. Where are we to worship God?
5. How would a future temple in Jerusalem undermine the finished work of Christ?

7. Overture to Armageddon: Want to be left behind?

What is the idea behind the 'rapture'?

The rapture is the novel idea that Jesus will actually return twice: first of all secretly, to rescue true believers out of the world, before or mid-way through a seven-year period of intense suffering known as the tribulation, then visibly with his saints to judge the world. So advocates claim Jesus will return secretly *for* his saints, then visibly *with* his saints. Although now a dominant view in America, largely as a result of Tim LaHaye's immensely popular *Left Behind*[1] series, the idea of a two-stage rapture (see Figure 7.1) has been traced to the eccentric views of

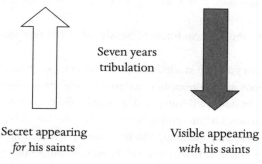

Seven years
tribulation

Secret appearing   Visible appearing
for his saints   *with* his saints

Figure 7.1. The two-stage rapture.

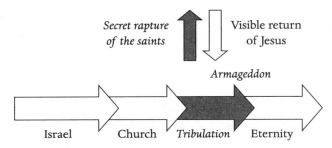

Figure 7.2. The rapture.

J. N. Darby and Cyrus Scofield.[2] To the traditional hope of the visible return of Jesus they added the notion of a secret return associated with a time of great suffering and persecution for those left behind on earth. Proponents believe that in one cataclysmic moment, millions of believers around the world will suddenly be caught up in the air to be with Jesus. Life will continue on earth for those who have ignored or rejected Jesus for either three and a half years or seven years. Mid-tribulationists believe Christians will be rescued half-way through the tribulation. Perhaps not surprisingly, the more popular pre-tribulationist view doesn't involve any suffering for Christians (see Figure 7.2).

Hal Lindsey speculates on how the rapture will be perceived from the perspective of the non-Christian left behind,

> There I was driving down the freeway and all of a sudden the place went crazy . . . cars going in all directions . . . and not one of them had a driver. I mean it was wild. I think we've got an invasion from outer space.[3]

According to the website Rapture Ready, after the rapture,

> The prophecy section in all Christian bookstores will be cleaned out, and you may need reservations to attend Sunday church services. Well, maybe not at all churches. The world will be in a state of supreme chaos, and out of this mess will arise the man who will have an answer to every question. This man, the Antichrist, will be the greatest salesman in history because he will sell the people the biggest lie ever. Satan will be so impressed with him that he will give this man

his full power. At the end of this Tribulation there will be a great war known as Armageddon and Jesus will return visibly, defeat the Anti-Christ and reign on earth for a thousand years.[4]

In a review of *End Times* written by John Walvoord, Jews for Jesus' website promises reassuringly,

> The end times can be happy and rewarding for Christians. The key is understanding them. With clarity, logic and conviction, this book dramatically explores world events in light of biblical prophecy, outlining the precepts of our faith. Written by one of the field's top experts, it is the definitive work on prophecy.[5]

Similarly, they advertise LaHaye's best-selling books in the *Left Behind* series:

> Thrilling end-time adventure looks at life on Earth following the Rapture. In one cataclysmic moment, millions around the globe disappear, vehicles careen out of control, loved ones vanish before your eyes, global chaos ensues ... You'll pick it up – but not put it down![6]

What does the Bible say about the rapture?

Cyrus Scofield, in the footnotes to his *Reference Bible*, has to contradict Jesus in order to perpetuate the notion of a secret rapture of the saints before his visible return. In Matthew 13, in the Parable of the Wheat and the Tares, Jesus explains that the tares will be removed first and destroyed, and then the wheat gathered. When the servants ask, 'Do you want us to go and pull the weeds up?', the master replies,

> Let both grow together until the harvest. At that time I will tell the harvesters: first collect the weeds and tie them in bundles to be burned; then gather the wheat and bring it into my barn.
> (Matthew 13:30).

Jesus is using an illustration to describe his return, and therefore we must not read too much into the detail. Nevertheless, Jesus says that his return will be associated both with destruction and deliverance, condemnation and vindication. In a footnote to this verse, however, Scofield reverses the order and separates what Jesus combines to ensure it fits with his presuppositions.

> The gathering of the tares into bundles for burning does not imply immediate judgment. At the end of this Age (v. 40) the tares are set apart for burning, but first the wheat is gathered into the barn.[7]

If there is any significance to the harvesting process in Jesus' parable, it is surely teaching the opposite to Scofield. Likewise in a footnote to Acts 1:11, Scofield ignores the promise made by the angel that everyone will see Jesus when he returns. Instead, he claims that after Jesus returns to take believers secretly to heaven, there will then be a 'national regathering' of Israel, the 'destruction of the present political world-system followed by world-wide Gentile conversion'.[8]

The most frequently cited passage to justify a two-stage rapture is 1 Thessalonians 4:15–17.

> According to the Lord's word, we tell you that we who are still alive, who are left till the coming of the Lord, will certainly not precede those who have fallen asleep. For the Lord himself will come down from heaven, with a loud command, with the voice of the archangel and with the trumpet call of God, and the dead in Christ will rise first. After that, we who are still alive and are left will be caught up together with them in the clouds to meet the Lord in the air. And so we will be with the Lord for ever.
>
> (1 Thessalonians 4:15–17)

In commenting on 1 Thessalonians 4:15, in his *Synopsis of the Books of the Bible*, Darby asserts:

> Observe, also, that this revelation gives another direction to the hope of the Thessalonians, because it distinguishes with much precision between our departure hence to join the Lord in the air, and our return to the earth with Him.[9]

Now can you find in these verses a two-stage return of Jesus, first secret then visible? With, as Darby suggests, 'much precision'? No, neither can I. Ironically, some proponents claim that only those who do 'see' it in these verses will be raptured. Maybe it's a case of 'seeing is believing'. Darby certainly regarded disinterest in his teaching on the rapture as a sign that the church was apostate and his own 'Assembly' elect. Following Darby's rejection of the mainline denominations, Hal Lindsey seems to share the same sectarian views (see Table 7.1).

J. N. Darby	Hal Lindsey
The rapture of the saints before the appearing of Christ, strange as it may appear to some, has nothing to say to the church, directly or exclusively; but as we form part of those caught up, it of course, interests us in the highest degree.[10]	I've said it before and I will no doubt say it again: When the Rapture occurs, many churches will not have to find a new pastor. That's how badly infected the modern church is with deceiving spirits.[11]

Table 7.1.

The passage from Thessalonians does teach a sequence to the return of Jesus (see Table 7.2). But it is not the one dispensationalists hold to:

The sequence to the return of Jesus in 1 Thessalonians 4

1. Jesus will return to earth (4:16).
2. His return will be associated with loud sounds (4:16).
3. The dead in Christ will be raised first (4:16).
4. Those believers still alive will be caught up to meet him in the air (4:17).
5. We will be with the Lord for ever (4:17).

Table 7.2.

Nothing in 1 Thessalonians, or in any other New Testament passage, teaches that Jesus will return secretly to take believers to heaven for seven years and then return with them to earth for another thousand years.

The most conclusive repudiation of the notion of a secret rapture, however, comes from Jesus himself in Matthew 24:30–31.

> At that time the sign of the Son of Man will appear in the sky, and all the peoples of the earth will mourn. They will see the Son of Man coming on the clouds of the sky, with power and great glory. And he will send his angels with a loud trumpet call, and they will gather his elect from the four winds, from one end of the heavens to the other. (Matthew 24:30–31)

Jesus is using vivid imagery from the Old Testament to describe his return. The great trumpet refers to the silver trumpets used to call God's people to worship (Numbers 10:1–10), and the four winds (Jeremiah 49:36; Zechariah 2:6) symbolize the entire world. In this way Jesus will gather his elect 'from every nation, tribe, people and language' (Revelation 7:9). The sequence in this passage is equally clear and reinforces that found in 1 Thessalonians (see Table 7.3).

The sequence to the return of Jesus in Matthew 24

---

1. There will be a sign of Jesus appear in the sky (24:30).
2. Jesus himself will appear visibly (24:30).
3. The whole world will see him and mourn (24:30).
4. The event will be accompanied by loud sounds (24:31).
5. Then Jesus will send his angels to gather his elect (24:31).

Table 7.3.

So believers will be caught up to be with Jesus when he returns visibly, not before. The whole world will be watching and mourning. What is certain from this passage is that the rapture will not occur before Jesus returns, and that nothing relating to the return of Jesus will be secret. Perhaps not surprisingly, there are no footnotes or comments to these important verses in either the *Scofield Reference Bible* or *The New Scofield Study Bible*.

Sadly, the mistaken idea of a secret rapture has generated a lot of bad theology. It is probably the reason why many Christians don't seem to care about climate change or about preserving diminishing supplies of natural resources. They are similarly not worried about the national debt, nuclear war, or world poverty, because they hope to be raptured to heaven and avoid suffering the consequences of the coming global holocaust. Like a sinking ship, the world is doomed. There is therefore no point in preserving the world or getting involved in charitable or humanitarian work. Every human tragedy, be it earthquake, hurricane or war, merely adds to the mounting evidence, proving their contention that the end of the world is nigh.[12]

The hype surrounding the *Left Behind* phenomenon is a tragic example of what happens when people major on minors and dogmatize on obscure verses. We must base our beliefs on the central truths of God's Word. I do not believe God has written off this beautiful world. Nor am I desperate to leave it. We have a mission to fulfil (Philippians 1:21–25). I am not the only one who will be happy to be 'left behind', at least until Jesus does return.[13]

The signs of the times

In a *Newsweek* article headed *Are These the End Times?*, Tim LaHaye was asked 'How do you interpret what's happening in the Middle East? Are you seeing signs that these are the end of days?' By now you should be able to predict what LaHaye had to say:

> Biblically speaking, the very nations that are mentioned in prophecy – and have been mentioned for 2,500 years as occupying the focus of the tension of the last days – are the very nations that are involved in the conflict right now. That may be one of the reasons there's a sudden interest in bible prophecy because all of a sudden they realize end-time events could possibly take place and break forth right now.[14]

While Jesus stated, 'about that day or hour no one knows' (Matthew 24:36), some of his followers today are at least trying, it seems, to predict the month. Visit the website of Rapture Ready and you can check out the Rapture Index. Over forty distinct signs are identified from the Scriptures, grouped under four headings: 'natural', 'social', religious' and 'prophetic'. Each sign is given a score based on its frequency, intensity or significance at any given moment in time. The combined scores are then totalled. Using this method of calculation, apparently anything over 150 means 'fasten your seatbelts'.[15]

I recently preached a sermon on Daniel 7 – 8 and speculated on possible ways in which this passage may contain 'signs' for our generation. Daniel gives us three clues that help us identify that this passage is talking about the present day.

1. 'As I watched, this horn was waging war against the holy people and defeating them' (Daniel 7:21). We are dealing with a time of great persecution of Christians. More Christians died in the twentieth century than in the previous nineteen centuries combined.
2. 'The ten horns are ten kings who will come from this kingdom' (Daniel 7:24). We must be dealing with events soon to take place because this configuration of ten nations has not yet happened in history.
3. ' "Son of man," he said to me, "understand that the vision concerns the time of the end . . . but seal up the vision, for it concerns the distant future" ' (Daniel 8:17, 26). These visions in Daniel 7 – 8 clearly refer to events close to the end of the world.

Where is this leading then? Think about it: before you can read a map you must first pin-point your present location on it. It is the same with prophecy. Daniel mentions four animals that represent four empires – the lion with eagle wings, the bear, the leopard, and a fourth, too awful to describe. Let's see if we can identify them. If we start with the last – we have already observed that the ten kingdoms have not yet emerged. This may describe a super confederation of the United States of Europe or possibly a new Islamic Confederacy emerging around Iran and Syria. If the fourth beast will rise in the near future we can easily name the other three. First, the lion. Which nation has the lion as its symbol? Dead right – Britain. At the beginning of the twentieth century, Britain had the largest empire in the world. One quarter of the world's population and one fifth of the world's land mass was part of the British Empire. What about the eagle wings? The USA, of course! Since the Second World War, the United States have taken over the role of Britain and become the world's only English-speaking superpower, but it is already in decline. So the first beast represents the British and American Empire. What of the bear? Which nation is symbolized by a bear? Russia, naturally. For nearly seventy years the Soviet communist Empire, aided by China, dominated the world. I can see you are getting into this now. So what about the leopard with four bird's wings and four heads? Did you know that the UN and G8 has divided the world into four sectors – the Americas, Asia, Europe and Africa – which will ultimately be ruled by four heads who will answer to the UN Security Council led by the Secretary General? When I preached this sermon, Tony Blair had just announced that he was standing down as leader of the Labour Party. I went on to say, 'And you know the leading candidate when the UN's Kofi Annan retires? Tony Blair . . . If Tony Blair does become the new UN Secretary General (or gets a job behind the scenes), we are assured of stronger powers for the UN, the use of pre-emptive force against countries defying UN resolutions, and a more united world. Have you read that somewhere before in the book of Revelation?'

OK – I need to make an apology. I have been leading you astray. I may not have actually convinced you, but I certainly convinced many of my congregation judging from the open mouths and wide eyes that day. You see how easy it is to play games with the biblical text? With a vivid imagination and a receptive audience it is not hard to 'prove' selected prophecies are coming true today. Go to the website of Rapture Ready and you will find a list of possible anti-Christ figures. In 2006, the list included Bill Gates, Tony Blair, Prince Charles and Kofi Annan.[16]

How then should we interpret the 'signs of the times'? Jesus said:

There will be signs in the sun, moon and stars. On the earth, nations will be in anguish and perplexity at the roaring and tossing of the sea. People will faint from terror, apprehensive of what is coming on the world, for the heavenly bodies will be shaken. At that time they will see the Son of Man coming in a cloud with power and great glory. When these things begin to take place, stand up and lift up your heads, because your redemption is drawing near.
(Luke 21:25–28)

Table 7.4 lists some generic signs to watch out for:

Type of sign	Manifestation	Bible reference
Geological	Great earthquakes	Luke 21:11
Biological	Plagues and famines	Luke 21:11
Political	Jerusalem under Gentile control	Luke 21:20–24
Military	Wars and rumours of wars	Mark 13:7–8
Moral	Lawlessness, violence and immorality	2 Timothy 3:1–5
Religious	Apostasy and false prophets	Matthew 24:10–13
Evangelistic	The gospel proclaimed to the whole world	Matthew 24:14

Table 7.4.

Now these signs have been evident since Jesus first described them. It is therefore reasonable to assume that Jesus wanted us to understand that the magnitude or frequency of these signs would increase before he returns, so that believers would recognize their significance. But the point is – they were never intended to tell us the time of Jesus' return.

Think of them like the hazard warning signs you see on a motorway. They keep you alert and ready for whatever lies ahead. They were never intended to be like mileage signs that tell you how far away you are from your destination. Jesus wants to keep us awake, not guessing. And anyway, the troubles and sorrows predicted by Jesus are not the end in themselves but only the 'birth pangs'. Ask any mother what that feels like. These signs merely precede the visible appearance of the Lord Jesus Christ. Nobody knows when Jesus will return. Two things are certain though. First, we are nearer to that day than ever before in history. And second, these signs certainly appear more evident in our generation than ever before. The whole point of the Parable of the Ten Virgins (Matthew 25:1–13) is that we are wise if we live as if Jesus is returning today. If the thought that Jesus is returning today would cause you to change your priorities, then you'd better change them.

Armageddon or 'I'm a geddin out o' here'

From the number of column inches devoted to the battle of Armageddon in books by prophecy experts like Tim LaHaye, John Walvoord and Hal Lindsey, you might be forgiven for thinking it must be a pretty important subject in the Bible. It comes as a bit of a surprise therefore to discover that *Har Megiddo* (the hill of Megiddo) gets only one mention in the entire New Testament (Revelation 16:13–20).

The *Scofield Bible* notes inform us that, 'Armageddon is the appointed place for the beginning of the great battle in which the Lord, at his coming in glory, will deliver the Jewish remnant besieged by the Gentile world-powers under the Beast and False Prophet.'[17]

Confident that Christians will escape and witness the events from the grandstands of heaven, exponents describe in graphic detail the suffering that will take place for unbelievers left on earth. Charles Ryrie, for example, predicts this will be, 'the time of Israel's greatest bloodbath'.[18] John Walvoord similarly predicts a holocaust in which at least 750 million people will perish.[19] Tim LaHaye warns that '"Jacob's trouble", prophesied by Jeremiah 30:7, will certainly be far worse than the Spanish Inquisition ... or even the Holocaust of Adolf Hitler.'[20] Not to be outdone, in *The Final Battle*, Hal Lindsey claims, 'Israel is in for a very rough time. The Jewish State will be brought to the brink of destruction.'[21] In a later chapter he clarifies what this will mean for the Jews:

> The land of Israel and the surrounding area will certainly be targeted for nuclear attack. Iran and all the Muslim nations around Israel have already been targeted with Israeli nukes ... All of Europe, the seat of power of the Antichrist, would surely be a nuclear battlefield, as would the United States ... Zechariah gives an unusual, detailed account of how hundreds of thousands of soldiers in the Israel battle zone will die. Their flesh will be consumed from their bones, their eyes from their sockets, and their tongues from their mouths while they stand on their feet (Zechariah 14:12). This is exactly the sort of thing that happens from the intense radiation of a neutron type bomb.[22]

John Hagee takes a similar line to Hal Lindsey over Iran. At the 19 July 2006 Washington DC inaugural event for Christians United for Israel, after a recorded greeting from George W. Bush, and in the presence of four US Senators and the Israeli ambassador to the US, John Hagee stated:

> The United States must join Israel in a pre-emptive military strike against Iran to fulfill God's plan for both Israel and the West ... a biblically prophesied end-time confrontation with Iran, which will lead to the Rapture, Tribulation, and Second Coming of Christ.[23]

Where Hagee justifies pre-emptive military action from Scripture is rather doubtful. Like Zechariah, the book of Revelation is fertile ground for ultra-literalists who believe an imminent nuclear holocaust is forecast. For example, in Revelation 14 we read:

> Another angel came out of the temple in heaven, and he too had a sharp sickle. Still another angel, who had charge of the fire, came from the altar and called in a loud voice to him who had the sharp sickle, 'Take your sharp sickle and gather the clusters of grapes from the earth's vine, because its grapes are ripe.' The angel swung his sickle on the earth, gathered its grapes and threw them into the great winepress of God's wrath. They were trampled in the winepress outside the city, and blood flowed out of the press, rising as high as the horses' bridles for a distance of 1,600 stadia.
> (Revelation 14:17–20)

Lindsey claims this describes the consequence of a nuclear holocaust. For a distance of 200 miles from the Valley of Jezreel, near Megiddo across to the Jordan Valley then down to the Dead Sea and on to the Gulf of Aqaba, he claims the entire valley will be filled with the debris of war and the bodies of animals and people, and, above all, blood.

> I have travelled the entire length of this valley ... It is almost impossible to imagine the valley covered with blood five feet high! Yet that is exactly what God predicts, and He always fulfils His Word. Some have asked, 'Wouldn't the blood coagulate and not flow?' Blood exposed to intense radiation doesn't coagulate ... Because of the intense radiation, blood will not coagulate. It will literally become a sea of blood five feet deep.[24]

While similar speculative interpretations are common among other end-times commentators, William Hendriksen offers an alternative and rather more rational explanation for the figures contained in this passage.

> In the picture that John sees, a lake of blood results. It is so deep that horses can swim in it. It spreads out in all directions to the extent of sixteen hundred stadia. Remember that four is the number of the universe and the earth. This is the judgment of the wicked. Ten is the number of completeness. So, sixteen hundred, which is the product of four times four, times ten times ten, would seem to indicate that this is the thoroughly complete judgment of the wicked. And the winepress of God's wrath was trodden down outside the Holy City![25]

So, while Revelation 16:14–16 may just possibly be describing a literal battle that will soon take place near Megiddo, it is more likely that John is describing the final cosmic overthrow of evil by almighty God.

The future assessed: but which one?

Historically, Christians have viewed the future differently depending on how they have interpreted the reference to a thousand years in Revelation 20:1–6.[26] Some take it literally as a period of time on earth, while others interpret it metaphorically as describing events from a heavenly perspective. It boils down to one of four options and you will find well-known Christians associated with each.

1. Amillennialism

Amillennialists believe Revelation 20 describes the present reign of Jesus Christ in heaven (Matthew 28:18–20). There will be no literal or physical kingdom on earth when Christ returns. The kingdom of God is present in the world now as Christ rules the church through his Word and the Spirit. When Christ returns, there will be a general resurrection of the dead, followed by the final judgment. He will reign with his saints over a recreated earth in eternity (see Figure 7.3). John Calvin and Louis Berkhof were amillennialists. For amillennialists, Revelation 20 is metaphorical.[27]

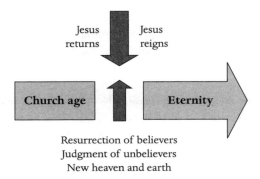

Figure 7.3. Amillennialism.

2. Postmillennialism

Postmillennialists believe that there will be an extended period of peace and prosperity on earth prior to the return of Christ. This is the millennium during which the gospel will be proclaimed to all nations, and Christian values will be universally embraced. When Christ returns, there will be a general resurrection of the dead followed by the final judgment. He will reign with his saints over a recreated earth in eternity (see Figure 7.4). Jonathan Edwards and George Whitfield were postmillennialists. For postmillennialists, Revelation 20 is symbolic.

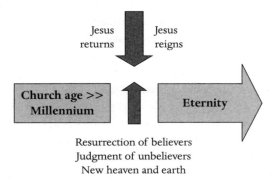

Figure 7.4. Postmillennialism.

3. Premillennialism

Premillennialists believe world events are leading to a climactic war and Christ will return to intervene. The first resurrection will occur and Christ will reign on earth in Jerusalem for a thousand years. At the end

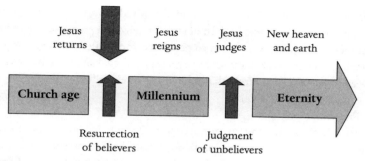

Figure 7.5. Premillennialism.

of the millennium, the last judgment will occur, Satan will be destroyed and the heavens and earth renewed. Christ's temporal kingdom will merge into his eternal kingdom (see Figure 7.5). There are two variants – covenantal and dispensational – depending on whether Israel and the church will share eternity together. Cyrus Scofield and Hal Lindsey are examples. For premillennialists, Revelation 20 is literal.

Those who see references to a millennium in Revelation 20:1–6 as metaphorical or symbolic (amillennial and post-millennial) tend to view the future positively. Those who believe Jesus will reign on earth for a thousand years (premillennial) tend to be pessimistic about future events prior to his return. Christian Zionists are invariably premillennialists and among the most pessimistic of all. Their highly speculative and imaginative interpretation of ancient prophecies has led many to believe that the restoration of Jews, the founding of the State of Israel, and conflict with the Arabs are all signs of the imminent return of Jesus. Grace Halsell observes:

> Convinced that a nuclear Armageddon is an inevitable event within the divine scheme of things, many evangelical dispensationalists have committed themselves to a course for Israel that, by their own admission, will lead directly to a holocaust indescribably more savage and widespread than any vision of carnage that could have generated in Adolf Hitler's criminal mind.[28]

Such a fatalistic view of the future, with its pre-written script, is inherently suspicious and pessimistic about anything international, ecumenical, or involving the European Community or United Nations.

Efforts to achieve a lasting peace in the Middle East are spurned as counterfeit and a satanic ploy to beguile Israel. Such paranoia might be deemed a sick joke, were it not so pervasive and influential, it seems, in shaping US foreign policy with its perpetual war against the 'axis of evil'. Its greatest danger is surely that it becomes a self-fulfilling prophecy.

4. Preterism

A fourth view gaining in popularity is known as preterism, from the Latin *praeter*, meaning 'past'. Preterists hold that some (partial preterists) or indeed all prophecy (full preterists) has been fulfilled in the generation that witnessed the death and resurrection of Jesus and the destruction of Jerusalem in AD 70. They take literally the promises Jesus made that his hearers would witness the events he predicted. In Matthew 16, for example, Jesus promised, 'Truly I tell you, some who are standing here will not taste death before they see the Son of Man coming in his kingdom' (Matthew 16:28; see also, Matthew 10:23; 23:35–36; 24:34; 26:63–64, for more examples). They point out, for instance, how the apocalyptic imagery found in Luke 21 of 'the heavenly bodies being shaken' when Jesus appears is remarkably similar to David's description of the defeat of Saul (Psalm 18:7–15), or Isaiah's prophecy against Babylon (Isaiah 13:1–19). In Matthew 24:21, Jesus promises the predicted destruction of Jerusalem is 'never to be equalled again', indicating that this cannot refer to the end of time. Preterists argue that when Jesus warned 'I am coming soon' (Revelation 2:16; 3:11; 22:7, 12, 20) he really meant it! Preterists include R. C. Sproul,[29] Gary DeMar[30] and John Noe.[31] Some preterists, such as Max and Tim King, describe their position as Transmillennialism.[32]

What does the Bible say about the return of Jesus?

Here are some promises from the New Testament to hold on to.

1. It will be a personal return (John 14:2–3)

2. It will be a visible return (Acts 1:9–11)

3. It will be an unmistakable return (Matthew 24:23–27, 30)

Jesus warns us against being 'taken in' by news that he has returned secretly or invisibly. His description should leave us in no doubt. 'For as lightning that comes from the east is visible even in the west, so will be the coming of the Son of Man' (Matthew 24:27). Furthermore, in Revelation 1:7, the apostle John promises, 'he is coming with the clouds, and every eye will see him.' So his return will be personal, visible and unmistakable.

4. It will be a sudden return (Mark 13:32–36)
Paul also emphasizes how sudden this event will be: 'In a flash, in the twinkling of an eye, at the last trumpet. For the trumpet will sound, the dead will be raised imperishable, and we will be changed' (1 Corinthians 15:52).

5. It will be an unexpected return (2 Peter 3:4, 10)
Peter also explains that some people will deny that Jesus is coming again. When Jesus came to earth the first time, he was not expected by the majority of people. It will be the same at his second coming. Jesus warned his disciples, 'for the Son of Man will come at an hour when you do not expect him' (Matthew 24:44). As for the unbelieving world, 'While people are saying "Peace and safety" then destruction will come on them suddenly' (1 Thessalonians 5:3).

6. It will be a glorious return (1 Thessalonians 4:16–17)
Jesus will return with the clouds (Revelation 1:7), with great power (Mark 13:36), and with his glorious angels (Matthew 16:27). In stark contrast to his first advent when he came as a vulnerable baby, Jesus will return in the full manifestation of his power.

Based on the New Testament, there are six things we can be sure about concerning the return of Jesus. It will be personal, visible, un-mistakable, sudden, unexpected and glorious.

How should we live in the light of Christ's return?
While there will always remain an element of mystery concerning the timing and precise details of our Lord's coming, he has told us enough to satisfy our faith, keep us watchful and assure us that he will return to take us to be with him where he reigns in glory. This is not our home.

But our citizenship is in heaven. And we eagerly await a Saviour from there, the Lord Jesus Christ, who, by the power that enables him to bring everything under his control, will transform our lowly bodies so that they will be like his glorious body.

(Philippians 3:20–21)

In Matthew 24, having explained that the hour of his return is unknown, Jesus challenges his followers to do three things.

Be watchful

'Therefore keep watch, because you do not know on what day your Lord will come' (Matthew 24:42). This means we must be vigilant, always aware that Jesus may return at any moment. We must constantly review our priorities, our choices and our actions in the light of Jesus' imminent return.

Be faithful

'Who then is the faithful and wise servant . . . ?' (Matthew 24:45). Jesus never commands us to be fruitful. He does command faithfulness. Faithfulness leads to fruitfulness. Faithful to what we already know of God's will for our lives. Faithful to the one who has called us, who saved us and who has gifted us.

Be serving

'It will be good for that servant whose master finds him doing so when he returns' (Matthew 24:46). We are told to be watchful, faithful and serving. Instead of speculating about the Lord's return, we have work to do – serving him according to the talents and gifts he has entrusted to us. Why? Because above all, Jesus has entrusted his mission to us. Which is? To make disciples – fully devoted followers of Jesus – of all nations. While we have time, let us use every opportunity God gives us to tell others how much God loves them. Jesus promises, 'Now that you know these things, you will be blessed if you do them' (John 13:17). Nearing the end of his life, the apostle Paul looked back over his life, first as an enemy of Christ, then as his servant, and expressed his hope for the future. 'Now there is in store for me the crown of righteousness, which the Lord, the righteous Judge, will award to me on that day – and not only to me, but also to all who have longed for his appearing' (2 Timothy 4:8). Are you looking forward to the return of Jesus? Do you long for his appearing? Is there unfinished business in your life? Then finish it quickly. Be ready before it is too late. Is there anything more important than Jesus in your life? Then it is too important. Revise your values before he has to, to your shame. If you knew that the Lord was returning tomorrow, would you change your priorities today? Then change them. Live today as if it were your last. Live as if it were yesterday that Christ died, as if he rose from the dead today, and as if he is coming back tomorrow. Then you will not be ashamed at his appearing, and you will not lose your reward. 'I am coming soon; hold on to what you have' (Revelation 3:11). Maranatha!

Chapter summary points

- The *Left Behind* phenomenon has created a destructive culture of pessimism and fatalism in Western Christianity.
- This polarized and apocalyptic world-view appears to be shaping US foreign policy in the Middle East and destabilizing the peace process.
- The idea of a secret two-stage rapture is a recent innovation without biblical foundation.
- The signs of the return of Christ are intended to keep us watchful, not tell us the time.
- Armageddon is not necessarily a reference to an apocalyptic nuclear holocaust, but the cosmic battle between good and evil.
- Jesus Christ will return personally, visibly, unmistakably, suddenly, unexpectedly and gloriously.
- In the light of his imminent return, we should be watchful and faithful servants doing his will.

Passages to review

Matthew 24:23–31; Mark 13:32–36; Luke 21:25–28; John 14:1–6; Acts 1:1–11; 1 Thessalonians 4:15–17; 2 Timothy 4:1–8; 2 Peter 3:4–10; Revelation 3:11; 7:9–16; 14:17–20; 16:13–20; 20:1–6.

Questions for further study

1. Why has the *Left Behind* craze gained such popularity?
2. How would you refute the idea of a secret rapture from Scripture?
3. What are the 'signs of the times'?
4. How should we interpret them?
5. How should we live in the light of the Lord's return?

Conclusions: The last word on the
8. Middle East?

Then I saw 'a new heaven and a new earth,' for the first heaven
and the first earth had passed away, and there was no longer any sea.
I saw the Holy City, the new Jerusalem, coming down out of heaven
from God, prepared as a bride beautifully dressed for her husband.
And I heard a loud voice from the throne saying, 'Look! God's
dwelling place is now among the people, and he will dwell with them.
They will be his people, and God himself will be with them and be
their God. "He will wipe every tear from their eyes. There will be no
more death" or mourning or crying or pain, for the old order of
things has passed away.' ... Then the angel showed me the river of the
water of life, as clear as crystal, flowing from the throne of God and of
the Lamb down the middle of the great street of the city. On each side
of the river stood the tree of life, bearing twelve crops of fruit, yielding
its fruit every month. And the leaves of the tree are for the healing of
the nations.
(Revelation 21:1–4; 22:1–2)

What is your vision of the future? However we understand the detail
of God's working in our world today, these verses describe where the
world is heading. This is God's purpose and therefore our mandate –

the healing of the nations. God's plan is nothing less than paradise restored. We look forward to the beauty, harmony and intimacy of a restored relationship between God and his people, where pain, suffering and death are no more. Is the way we view Israel and the church assisting or hindering God's plan? Are we furthering the biblical mandate to proclaim the gospel to Jew and Gentile, or have we substituted 'another' gospel? Are we 'doing justice and loving mercy' in the Middle East, or are we exacerbating tensions? Are we walking in the way of peace or are we hindering reconciliation between Arabs and Israelis?

What have we found so far?

In Chapter 1, we considered the significance of our presuppositions and their influence on our understanding of the Bible. We introduced the relationship between Israel and the church by comparing and contrasting two major theological positions, covenantalism and dispensationalism, setting the scene by refuting some of the red herrings used to discredit those who challenge Zion's Christian soldiers (Matthew 22:29).

In Chapter 2, we recognized the importance of reading the Bible literally and contextually. We explored the relationship between the old and new covenants, and saw how there is not only an organic unity, but also a clear and irreversible transition from the old to the new. We noted how the prophetic and apocalyptic books like Daniel and Revelation need careful handling to avoid erroneous interpretations. We saw how important it is that we resist taking contemporary events to be the realization of biblical prophecy. Instead, as we read the Bible, we must ask how a particular passage fits within God's progressive revelation and points to God's purposes revealed fully and finally in Jesus Christ (Luke 24:27).

In Chapter 3, we discovered that God has only ever had one 'chosen' people. Citizenship has always been inclusive and spiritual, never exclusive and physical, despite human efforts to make it so. Membership was always on the basis of grace through faith, not race or ritual. The church of Jesus Christ, or the Israel of God, includes both the Old Testament saints as well as the New Testament saints. All who looked forward to the coming of their Saviour, as much as those who recognized Jesus when he came, are the true children of

Abraham and Sarah. The promises made to Abraham have been fulfilled in and through the church. The beautiful imagery used to describe God's people in the Old Testament is repeatedly applied to God's people in the New Testament. When Jesus died on the cross, he broke down the wall of separation between Jewish and Gentile believers, making one new humanity and reconciling both to God in himself (Ephesians 2:15–16).

In Chapter 4, we surveyed the purpose and extent of the Promised Land. We saw that the land always belonged to God. His people were only ever strangers and tenants with, at best, temporary residence. Their presence in the land was always conditional on faithful obedience. Unfaithfulness led to exile in Assyria and Babylon. Repentance led to restoration. God's kingdom on earth was always international. Jesus redefined the concept of the kingdom as a spiritual and heavenly reality that encompasses his faithful servants of all nations. Jesus repudiated the notion of an earthly and nationalistic kingdom. His disciples looked forward to a better and more secure inheritance (Hebrews 11:16).

In Chapter 5, we considered the place of Jerusalem in God's purposes. Far from being an exclusive capital for the Jewish people, we discovered that the Old Testament vision is of a city that is intended to be inclusive and a focus for all nations. In the New Testament, Jerusalem becomes associated increasingly with the death and resurrection of Jesus. We considered the meaning of the ending of 'the times of the Gentiles', and recognized that this best describes the period before the return of Jesus. Thoughts of national sovereignty are eclipsed by images of the heavenly Jerusalem, which is the true home of all who trust in Christ (Galatians 4:26).

In Chapter 6, we thought about the temple and considered its role in teaching people about the history of salvation, the seriousness of sin and the need for sacrifice. That is why we remained unconvinced by the arguments for a new temple in Jerusalem. The language used to describe the temple of the 'living God' (2 Corinthians 6:16) is now applied to the church, with Jesus as the cornerstone, and his followers as the 'living stones' that form it. When Jesus died to atone for our sins, the temple in Jerusalem became redundant.

In Chapter 7, we faced the logical consequences of Christian Zionism, which is inherently pessimistic about the future. This is because it is based on assumptions about the Jewish people, the land, Jerusalem and the temple, which are drawn almost exclusively from the 'shadows' of the Old Testament rather than the 'light' of the New Testament. They do not take account of the way these concepts are fulfilled, replaced, annulled, expanded or given new definition by Jesus and the apostles. How we should view the future is a matter on which

	Old Testament promise	New Testament fulfilment
God's people	Genesis 12:3	Galatians 3:16, 29
	Genesis 22:17	Revelation 5:9
	Isaiah 5:1–7	Matthew 21:33–41
	Psalm 80	John 15
	Deuteronomy 18:19	Acts 3:23
	Amos 9:11–12	Acts 15:14–19
	Hosea 1:10; 2:23	Romans 9:21–26
	Genesis 21:10	Galatians 4:30
God's land	Psalm 37:11	Matthew 5:5
	Genesis 12:3; 22:18; 26:4; 28:14	Acts 3:24–25
	Deuteronomy 5:16	Ephesians 6:1–3
	Genesis 23:4; 1 Chronicles 29:15	1 Peter 1
God's city	Jeremiah 12:7; 22:5	Luke 13:34–35
	Isaiah 29:3; Ezekiel 4:2	Luke 19:41–44
	Isaiah 63:3–6	Luke 21:24
	Isaiah 54:1	Galatians 4:26–27
	Isaiah 52:1	Revelation 21:2, 22–26
God's temple	2 Samuel 7:5–7	John 2:19–21
	Psalm 40:6–8	Hebrews 10:1–10
	Leviticus 26:12; Isaiah 52:11	2 Corinthians 6:16–17
	Psalm 118:22; Isaiah 28:16	1 Peter 2:5–7

Table 8.1.

godly Christians are wise not to be dogmatic. We noted that the role of the 'signs' of Jesus' return are to keep us alert, not to enable us to tell the time. References to Armageddon do not necessarily lock us into believing there has to be an apocalyptic war between Islam and Christianity. While the idea of a two-stage rapture is entirely fictional, the return of Jesus is not. It will be personal, visible, unmistakable and sudden. Jesus is coming back! Our role, as his servants, is to be watchful and faithful (Matthew 24:45).

Table 8.1 summarizes these findings. It shows that in terms of identifying God's people, in terms of the significance of the land, the centrality of Jerusalem and the importance of the temple, Old Testament type and shadow give way to New Testament reality. In each aspect the hopes and expectations of the old covenant have been fulfilled in the new covenant, fully and finally in the person of Jesus Christ.

In his helpful book, *God's Big Picture*, Vaughan Roberts traces the story-line of the Bible.[1] He shows how God's plan of redemption, using the imagery of the King and his kingdom, is revealed progressively from Genesis to Revelation as a 'binding theme of the whole Bible'.[2] Citing Graeme Goldsworthy, Roberts explains the concept of the kingdom as 'God's people in God's place under God's rule and blessing'.[3] Table 8.2 is adapted from his book and summarizes what we have discovered about the continuity between Israel and the church. It also shows the progression from Old Testament promise to New Testament fulfilment. In each phase of God's redemptive plan, notice the unique role which the Lord Jesus Christ has fulfilled in bringing our redemption to completion.

What difference has Jesus made?

The fundamental question we have considered in this book is this: What difference did the coming of Jesus Christ make to the traditional Jewish hopes and expectations? Was it the fulfilment or merely the postponement of those hopes?

Remember this is not a new controversy. In the first century, Christians debated the relationship between Israel and the church. The book of Hebrews is all about the relationship between the old and new covenants and how Jesus fulfilled the first in order to inaugurate the second.

The kingdom of God	God's people	God's place	God's purposes	God's Son	God's Word
The pattern of the kingdom	Adam and Eve	Garden of Eden	Perfect relationship	Creator (John 1:3)	Genesis 1 – 2
The perished kingdom	Pre-Abraham	Banished	Broken relationship	Offspring (John 8:56)	Genesis 3 – 11
The promised kingdom	Abraham and his descendants	Wandering	Covenant relationship	Bronze snake (John 3:14)	Genesis 12 – Deuteronomy
The partial kingdom	Israel from Joshua to Solomon	Canaan	Obedient relationship	Son of David (John 7:42)	Joshua – 2 Chronicles 9
The prophesied kingdom	The exiles	Captivity	Repentant relationship	The Son of God (John 8:31–58)	2 Chronicles 10 – Malachi
The present kingdom	The disciples	True temple	Justified relationship	Passover Lamb of God (John 1:29)	Matthew – John
The proclaimed kingdom	The church	World	Renewed relationship	Saviour of the world (John 4:42)	Acts – Revelation 3
The perfected kingdom	Every nation, tribe, people and language	New heaven and earth	Blessed relationship	Lord (John 20:28)	Revelation 4 – 21

Table 8.2.

Therefore, holy brothers and sisters, who share in the heavenly calling, fix your thoughts on Jesus, whom we acknowledge as our apostle and high priest. He was faithful to the one who appointed him, just as Moses was faithful in all God's house. Jesus has been found worthy of greater honour than Moses, just as the builder of a house has greater honour than the house itself. For every house is built by someone, but God is the builder of everything. 'Moses was faithful as a servant in all God's house,' bearing witness to what would be spoken by God in the future. But Christ is faithful as the Son over God's house. And we are his house, if indeed we hold firmly to our confidence and the hope in which we glory.

(Hebrews 3:1–6)

The writer of Hebrews develops this argument in chapter 4. In an overview of Jewish history, the progressive revelation of God's 'rest' points to, and then beyond, Canaan. It begins with God resting on the seventh day of creation (Hebrews 4:3–4). Because of their rebellion in the desert, God denied the adults access to the land (4:5). Once in the land, even the 'rest' from their enemies achieved under Joshua was provisional (4:8). Psalm 95 is quoted to indicate a future rest beyond even the zenith of the kingdom achieved under David (4:6–7). Believers are urged to look forward to and enter a more permanent rest than provided in Canaan.

There remains, then, a Sabbath-rest for the people of God; for those who enter God's rest also rest from their own work, just as God did from his. Let us, therefore, make every effort to enter that rest, so that no-one will perish by following their example of disobedience.
(Hebrews 4:9–11)

Craig Blomberg provides a helpful illustration showing the progression from creation to Christ in these verses[4] (see Figure 8.1).

Clearly, Orthodox Jews who do not yet recognize Jesus as their Messiah still have their eyes fixed on Moses, adhere to the demands of the law and cling to the promises of a literal inheritance in the land. Christians who identify with Zionism and believe the Old Testament promises the land, Jerusalem and the temple to the Jewish people in perpetuity are in danger of doing the same.

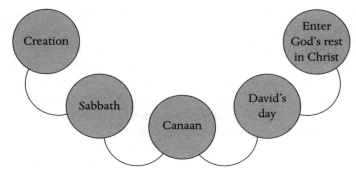

Figure 8.1. Entering God's rest in Hebrews.

Hebrews 6 explains that the progression from the old to the new covenant, which was consummated in the death of Jesus, our ransom sacrifice, is irreversible.

> It is impossible for those who have once been enlightened, who have tasted the heavenly gift, who have shared in the Holy Spirit, who have tasted the goodness of the word of God and the powers of the coming age and who have fallen away, to be brought back to repentance. To their loss they are crucifying the Son of God all over again and subjecting him to public disgrace.
> (Hebrews 6:4–6)

This is because, 'We have this hope as an anchor for the soul, firm and secure. It enters the inner sanctuary behind the curtain, where our forerunner, Jesus, has entered on our behalf. He has become a high priest for ever, in the order of Melchizedek' (Hebrews 6:19–20). Faith in Jesus Christ, as the consummation of all the hopes of Israel, is the highest spiritual mountain top beyond which it is downhill whichever way a person goes. There is nothing greater, nothing higher, and certainly nothing more magnificent than the mountain top of divine revelation found in the Lord Jesus Christ. David Breese describes the alternatives:

> To move beyond that mountain top in the pursuit of something better is to lose oneself in the crags and crevices of the slopes that fall away from real Christianity. And beyond the crevices of heresy are the fever

swamps of the cults, where the serpents and the scorpions wait. Beyond rationality is insanity, beyond medicine is poison, beyond sex is perversion, beyond fascination is addiction, beyond love is lust, beyond reality is fantasy. Just so, beyond Christianity is death, hopelessness, darkness, and heresy.[5]

As we have already seen, one verse in Hebrews sums up the relationship between the old and new covenants. 'By calling this covenant "new", he has made the first one obsolete; and what is obsolete and outdated will soon disappear' (Hebrews 8:13). The destruction of the temple with its holy of holies and altar, the death of the high priest, the dispersion of the Levites and the ending of animal sacrifices in AD 70, fulfilled that prediction. The choice since then has been between two theologies: one based primarily on the fading shadows of the old covenant and one based on the reality of the new covenant.

How then does the Old Testament relate to Jesus?

Graeme Goldsworthy's book, *According to Plan*, includes a simple but effective diagram, showing the relationship of the Old Testament to Christ, together with some New Testament assessments[6] (see Table 8.3). The Bible passages cited in this adaptation show conclusively that the Old Testament imagery, and the promises associated with it,

Old Testament	Jesus Christ	Scripture reference
Prophetic word	Completed	Hebrews 1:1–2
All prophecy	Fulfilled	Acts 13:32–33
All God's promises	Yes	2 Corinthians 1:20
David's line	Ended	Romans 1:3
Promise to David	Answered	Acts 2:30–31
Mystery of salvation	Revealed	Ephesians 3:3–6
Sacrifices	Finished	Hebrews 10:11–12
Eternal purposes	Accomplished	Ephesians 3:11
Whole Old Testament	Concerning	Luke 24:27

Table 8.3.

cannot be applied to the Jewish people and Judaism today, as if the coming of Jesus merely resulted in the postponement of those promises. They were fully and finally accomplished in Jesus Christ (John 5:39).

The fulfilment in Christ of the Old Testament promises concerning the land, the law and temple is best articulated in Stephen's sermon in Acts 6 – 7. His 'Old Testament survey' not only refutes the serious charges laid against him concerning the temple and the law, but points to Jesus as the fulfilment of both (Acts 6:12–14).

1. The land (Acts 7:1–18): Stephen begins by reminding his listeners that while the Patriarchs were faithful, none received an inheritance in the Promised Land.
2. The law (Acts 7:18–43): Stephen reviews the life of Moses and alludes to the coming of another prophet whom the people should follow. Clearly his intent was to show that Jesus was the person Moses promised, and that his message should be heeded.
3. The temple (Acts 7:44–50): Stephen's sermon moved from the land and law to the most sensitive issue – the temple. He points out that God had originally lived with his people in a portable tabernacle. When, like the surrounding nations, they wanted a king and temple, God acquiesced. Stephen quotes from Isaiah 66 to show that God anticipated the dangers associated with an immovable temple (Acts 7:48–50).

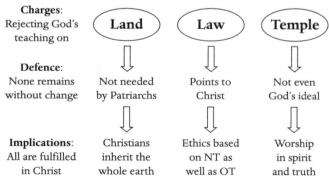

Figure 8.2. Stephen's breakthrough (Acts 6 – 7).

Through his sermon, Stephen turns the tables on them and shows that it is they who were lawbreakers, not him. Craig Blomberg has produced an illuminating chart (see Figure 8.2) that highlights the charges against Stephen, his defence and implications for Christians.[7]

Digging deeper

If you want to delve further into the origins of this controversy, get hold of my book, *Christian Zionism: Road-map to Armageddon?* (IVP, 2004). It does three things. First, it traces the history of the movement, identifying the various strands of its family tree on both sides of the Atlantic. Second, it explores the theology of the movement and how the Bible is used and abused. Third, it examines the political agenda of Christian Zionism, and that's where it gets really scary. There are literally hundreds of organizations dedicated to realizing the Zionist agenda. Now do you see how what we believe affects how we behave?

If you would like to study this further or receive regular updates, check out www.christianzionism.org and my own website www.sizers.org for more articles, audio and video material.

'The Jerusalem Declaration on Christian Zionism' is an historic document that was issued by the heads of the mainline denominations in Jerusalem in 2006 as an urgent plea for help from the worldwide church to counter the destructive effects of Christian Zionism. Living in close proximity to Jews and Muslims, they experience its negative impact on a daily basis. In the eyes of many Muslims, Christianity is increasingly equated with one-sided diplomatic support for Israel and aggressive military action in the Middle East. This is not only fuelling tension between the West and Islam, but is also endangering the very existence of the church in Israel and Palestine. The text of the document may be found on the websites mentioned above.

I am honoured that we have John Stott's permission to include an unpublished sermon he once delivered at All Souls Church, Langham Place, London. Entitled 'The Place of Israel', it provides an erudite and succinct analysis of the controversy from a biblical perspective.

Now that you know these things

In this book we have focused on biblical passages that speak about God's people, the land, Jerusalem, the temple and the future. By now you will have figured out why I believe Christian Zionism to be a defective, misguided and sometimes dangerous theology.

What David J. Bosch, the missions expert, writes about Hal Lindsey's theology could justifiably serve as an epitaph for a much wider genre of Christian Zionism:

> Lindsey's descriptions of the future are deterministic in the extreme; his apocalyptic is devoid of a Christological focus; the biblical materials he cites are totally divorced from their proper historical contexts; his hope for the future is self-centered in the extreme; and there is no theology of the cross in his apocalyptic.[8]

When you distil it down, what are you left with? An exclusive theology driving a political agenda which elevates one nation over others, rather than an inclusive theology centred on Jesus Christ, the Saviour of the world. In its worst forms, Christian Zionism uses the Bible to justify racial superiority, land expropriation, home demolitions, population transfer, colonial settlements, the denial of international law and the dehumanization of Arabs. It fuels not only Islamophobia but also anti-Semitism and Islamist retaliation against Christians. What does Jesus think about all this? On Palm Sunday, Luke tells us, 'As he approached Jerusalem and saw the city, he wept over it and said, "If you, even you, had only known on this day what would bring you peace – but now it is hidden from your eyes"' (Luke 19:41–42). I believe Jesus continues to weep not only over Jerusalem, a city whose very name means 'peace', but also for his children who promote a theology of war and conquest. It all seems a very long way from the simple teaching of Jesus, who promised, 'Blessed are the peacemakers for they will be called children of God' (Matthew 5:9). There are three simple ways we can demonstrate our paternity, diffuse tensions between Jews, Christians and Muslims, and contribute to justice, peace and reconciliation.

1. Pray for the peace of Jerusalem

> Pray for the peace of Jerusalem:
> 'May those who love you be secure.

> May there be peace within your walls
>> and security within your citadels.'
> For the sake of my friends and of all the people,
>> I will say, 'Peace be within you.'
> (Psalm 122:6–8).

2. Seek peace and pursue it

Do not repay evil with evil or insult with insult. On the contrary, repay evil with blessing, because to this you were called so that you may inherit a blessing. For,

> 'Whoever among you would love life
>> and see good days
> must keep your tongue from evil
>> and your lips from deceitful speech.
> Turn from evil and do good;
>> seek peace and pursue it.'
> (1 Peter 3:9–11; Psalm 34:12–16)

3. Proclaim the Prince of Peace

I am not ashamed of the gospel, because it is the power of God that brings salvation to everyone who believes: first to the Jew, then to the Gentile. For in the gospel the righteousness of God is revealed – a righteousness that is by faith from first to last, just as it is written: 'The righteous will live by faith.'
(Romans 1:16–17; Habakkuk 2:4)

Jesus said, 'Now that you know these things, you will be blessed if you do them' (John 13:17).

The Place of Israel

John Stott, Rector Emeritus of All Souls Church, Langham Place, London

The topic assigned to me is 'the place of Israel'. It is an object lesson in biblical hermeneutics, i.e. in how to interpret Scripture. For there are at least four ways in which the word 'Israel' may be used.

1. 'Israel' was that devious scoundrel, the younger son of Isaac and Rebekah. His first name was 'Jacob' (meaning 'he who deceives' or 'he who supplants'), and he amply lived up to this name. But God re-named him 'Israel' (meaning 'he who strives with God') because, having struggled with men all his life, he came at last to struggle with God for the blessing he wanted, although he was not entitled to it.

2. 'Israel' was the chosen, covenant people of God in Old Testament days, namely the twelve tribes descended from the twelve sons of Jacob. They were commonly known as 'the children of Israel' because Israel (i.e. Jacob) was their common ancestor.

3. 'Israel' is the Messianic community, the people of Jesus, the true descendants of Abraham because they share Abraham's faith. 'If you belong to Christ,' Paul wrote, 'then you are Abraham's seed, and heirs according to the promise' (Galatians 3:29). So this includes Gentiles who believe in Jesus, but excludes Jews who

do not. When Paul ended his letter to the Galatians with the words 'Peace and mercy ... to the Israel of God' (Galatians 6:16), he was referring to believers in Jesus, irrespective of their ethnic origin.

4. 'Israel' today for most people means the Israeli nation. Promised a national home by the Balfour Declaration of 1917, they were given it in 1948.

Thus 'Israel' has four distinct meanings. It means Jacob. It means Jews. It means Christians. And it means Israelis.

To which of these four meanings are we referring, then, when we ask about 'the place of Israel' in the purpose of God? Perhaps the best way to answer this question is to concentrate (as the Bible does) on the second and third meanings, and to consider Israel's past, present and future.

1. Israel's past

Old Testament Israel was God's 'chosen' and 'covenant' people. God's covenant promise to Abraham, later renewed to Isaac and Jacob, was: 'I will be your God, and you shall be my people.' True, for some 400 years of Egyptian slavery God appeared to have forgotten his covenant. But then at last we read: 'The Israelites groaned in their slavery, and ... God heard their groaning and he remembered his covenant with Abraham, with Isaac and with Jacob. So God looked on the Israelites and was concerned about them' (Exodus 2:23–25).

In consequence, God rescued his people, and about three months later at Mount Sinai God said to them:

You yourselves have seen ... how I carried you on eagles' wings and brought you to myself. Now if you obey me fully and keep my covenant, then out of all nations you will be my treasured possession. Although the whole earth is mine, you will be for me a kingdom of priests and a holy nation.'
(Exodus 19:4–6)

The people of Israel never forgot those promises or that covenant. Their literature (i.e. the Old Testament) is full of expressions of wonder that God should have called and chosen them, that he should have had mercy on them and entered into a solemn but gracious covenant with them.

For example, here are five rhetorical questions asked by Moses:

'What other nation is so great as to have their gods near them the way the LORD our God is near us whenever we pray to him?'
(Deuteronomy 4:7)

'And what other nation is so great as to have such righteous decrees and laws as this body of laws I am setting before you today?'
(Deuteronomy 4:8)

'Has anything so great as this ever happened, or has anything like it ever been heard of?'
(Deuteronomy 4:32)

'Has any other people heard the voice of God speaking out of fire, as you have, and lived?'
(Deuteronomy 4:33)

'Has any god ever tried to take for himself one nation out of another nation, by testings, by miraculous signs and wonders, by war, by a mighty hand and an outstretched arm, or by great and awesome deeds, like all the things the LORD your God did for you in Egypt before your very eyes?'
(Deuteronomy 4:34)

Then to these rhetorical questions other passages of Scripture add statements, which in the same way affirm the uniqueness of Israel:

The LORD did not set his affection on you and choose you because you were more numerous than other peoples, for you were the fewest of all peoples. But it was because the LORD loved you and kept the oath he swore to your forefathers that he brought you out with a mighty hand and redeemed you . . .
(Deuteronomy 7:7–8)

Again, 'He has revealed his word to Jacob, his laws and decrees to Israel. He has done this for no other nation; they do not know his laws'

(Psalm 147:19–20). Israel's sense of unique privilege permeates the Old Testament.

In the New Testament, Paul gives a list of eight particular privileges which distinguished the people of Israel. Theirs alone, he writes, are:

1. 'the adoption of sons' (because God adopted the nation as his son)
2. 'the divine glory' (the shining symbol of God's presence in the holy of holies)
3. 'the covenants' (by which he pledged himself to be their God)
4. 'the receiving of the law' (also called 'the oracles of God', the revelation of God's will)
5. 'the temple worship' (both the sacrifices that prefigured Jesus and the psalms we use in worship today)
6. 'the promises' (especially of the Messiah's coming kingdom)
7. 'the patriarchs' (whose stories are told in Genesis)
8. 'the human ancestry of Christ' ('who is God over all') (Romans 9:4–5)

No wonder the apostle also says that he has 'great sorrow and unceasing anguish' in his heart for his people. He could wish even to be himself cursed and cut off from Christ if only thereby his people might be saved (Romans 9:2–3).

Away then with anti-Semitism! It has been an appalling scandal in the history of Europe, and even the Christian church has been implicated. Christians should be 'pro-Semitic', in the sense that we recognize how the people of Israel have been highly favoured by God. We Gentiles are their debtors, Paul wrote (Romans 15:27). We owe them a huge spiritual debt, especially in their bequest to the world of both the Scriptures and the Christ.

2. Israel's present

Who, then, according to the New Testament perspective, is Israel today? The answer will have enormously surprised most of its readers, and still surprises many today. It is that true Israel is neither Jews nor Israelis, but believers in the Messiah.

We begin to trace this theme in the Old Testament. For already in the Old Testament, physical descent from Abraham, Isaac and Jacob was not regarded as enough. Many people thought it was, misinterpreting election as favouritism. But the prophets taught that God's people were not immune to God's judgment. When through Amos God began his statement 'you only have I chosen of all the families of the earth', the people will confidently have anticipated the conclusion 'therefore I will protect you'. They will have been thunderstruck when instead God concluded 'therefore I will punish you for all your sins' (Amos 3:2, emphasis added).

More and more, as the years passed, the prophets drew a distinction between Israel as a whole, the faithless nation, and Israel the faithful remnant within the nation.

Then John the Baptist, the last Old Testament prophet, taught the positive counterpart to this distinction. Not only are there some Israelites who are not true Israel, but there are some who are not Israelites who nevertheless belong to true Israel. The Baptist said to the crowds who came to him: 'Do not begin to say to yourselves, "We have Abraham as our father." For I tell you that out of these stones God can raise up children for Abraham' (Luke 3:8). In the end, God did not produce children to Abraham out of stones, but he did out of Gentiles. Jesus stunned his contemporaries by declaring: 'I say to you that many will come from the east and the west [i.e. from the nations] and will take their places at the feast with Abraham, Isaac and Jacob in the kingdom of heaven', while 'the subjects of the kingdom will be thrown outside, into the darkness, where there will be weeping and gnashing of teeth' (Matthew 8:11–12).

It was Paul, however, as the commissioned apostle to the Gentiles, to whom God gave the full revelation of this amazing development. 'A man is not a Jew if he is only one outwardly', he wrote, 'nor is circumcision merely outward and physical'. On the contrary, 'a man is a Jew if he is one inwardly; and circumcision is circumcision of the heart, by the Spirit, not by the written code' (Romans 2:28, 29). Similarly, 'not all who are descended from Israel are Israel' (Romans 9:6). Again, 'it is we who are the circumcision, we who worship by the Spirit of God, who glory in Christ Jesus, and who put no confidence in the flesh' (Philippians 3:3).

The apostle Peter also makes the same affirmation. With extraordinary God-given audacity he takes the words of Exodus 19:4–6, which applied to the old Israel and re-applies them to the Christian community. He calls them both 'a holy priesthood' and 'a chosen people, a royal priesthood, a holy nation, a people belonging to God' (1 Peter 2:5, 9).

So then, paradoxical as it may seem, the true Jews today are Christians, and the true circumcision is that heart-change called new birth. The Gentile followers of Jesus who acknowledge him as the Messiah are more truly the people of Israel than those people of Israel who reject him.

How can this identification be justified? Only because we are 'in Christ'. God had promised to bless the nations through Abraham's seed (Genesis 12:1–3), and that seed is Christ. Both the Gospels' genealogies trace the human ancestry of Jesus to Abraham. Therefore the promised blessing is given to all who are in Christ, and the way to be 'in Christ' is not by birth but by rebirth, not physically by descent but spiritually by faith. 'Abraham . . . is the father of all who believe', whether they are circumcised or uncircumcised, that is, whether they are Jews or Gentiles (Romans 4:11, 12). Again, 'if you belong to Christ, then you are Abraham's seed, and heirs according to the promise' (Galatians 3:29).

This is why we who believe in Jesus read the Old Testament as *our* Scriptures, sing the Old Testament psalms as expressing *our* worship, and claim the Old Testament promises as applying to *us*. For all God's promises are fulfilled in Christ, and we are in Christ (2 Corinthians 1:20).

So far, we have considered (1) that in olden days 'Israel' was a *physical* designation, meaning the descendants of Jacob, and (2) that today 'Israel' is a *spiritual* designation, meaning believers in Jesus, whether they are descended from Jacob or not. This brings us to the third point.

3. Israel's future

If 'Israel' meant descendants of Jacob in the Old Testament and means believers in Jesus in the New Testament, must we conclude that God has no special future for physical Israel? That was the very question which Paul's teaching prompted Jewish objectors to ask. 'Did God reject his people?' (Romans 11:1). Moreover, two answers are given to the question, each beginning with the emphatic negative 'by no means!', 'not at all!' or 'God forbid!' (Romans 11:1, 11).

First, Paul writes: 'I am an Israelite myself.' It is clear, therefore, that 'God did not reject his people' (Romans 11:1, 2). On the contrary, a faithful remnant survived, who were both descendants of Jacob and believers in Jesus. We meet many of them in the New Testament, in addition to Paul. For all the first Christians were Jews, and there are many Hebrew Christians today. What then about those other descendants of Jacob who do not believe in Jesus? This issue prompted Paul's second question.

Secondly, 'did they stumble so as to fall beyond recovery?' (Romans 11:11). The answer again is 'not at all!' or 'by no means!' For God's rejection of them was not final, since their rejection of Christ was not final.

In order to illustrate this, Paul now develops in Romans 11 his allegory of two olive trees – a cultivated one (representing the Jewish people) and a wild one (representing the Gentile nations). According to verse 17, some branches of the cultivated tree have been broken off (unbelieving Jews), while in their place a slip from a wild olive has been grafted in (Gentile believers).

But one day those olive branches which have been broken off will be grafted back in again (verse 24).

> After all, if you were cut out of an olive tree that is wild by nature, and contrary to nature were grafted into a cultivated olive tree, how much more readily will these, the natural branches, be grafted back into their own olive tree!
>
> I do not want you to be ignorant of this mystery, brothers, so that you may not be conceited: Israel has experienced a hardening in part until the full number of the Gentiles has come in. And so all Israel will be saved ... (Romans 11:24–26b)

In other words, the hardening of Israel is only temporary. Later, Paul seems to be saying, there will be a widespread turning of Jews to Christ.

What then about the Promised Land? Is the setting up of the State of Israel a fulfilment of prophecy? Many think so, especially so-called 'dispensationalists'. Their argument is (a) that the prophets promised that Israel would return to the land, (b) that they delineated its boundaries, and (c) that since these promises were not fulfilled literally at the time, they must still be fulfilled in the future.

Others (among whom I include myself), however, do not hold this view. Why is this? I leave aside *political* considerations, for example, the grave injustices that have been done to the Palestinians and the risk of further Israeli expansionism (since the land promised to Abraham includes territory now belonging to Jordan, Lebanon and Syria). I concentrate instead on three *biblical* arguments about the Old Testament promises.

First, the Old Testament promises about the Jews' return to the land were accompanied by the promise that they would also return to the Lord. It is hard to see how the secular State of Israel can be a fulfilment of those prophecies.

Secondly, the Old Testament promises about the land are nowhere repeated in the New Testament. The prediction of Romans 11 is that many Jews will return to Christ; a return to the land is not mentioned. Only one New Testament verse can be claimed as referring to the land, namely Luke 21:24. Here Jesus said that 'Jerusalem will be trampled on by the Gentiles until the times of the Gentiles are fulfilled.' Some interpreters understand this as a promise that Jerusalem will one day be liberated from Gentile rule. But the word 'until' does not necessarily imply this. 'The times of the Gentiles' may refer not to the period of Gentile domination, after which Jerusalem will be free, but to the whole present world order, after which Christ will come in glory.

Thirdly, the Old Testament promises, according to the apostles, are fulfilled in Christ and in his new international community. The New Testament writers apply to Christ both the promise of the seed and the promise of the land. A return to Jewish nationalism would be incompatible with this New Testament perspective.

We have surveyed the biblical perspective on 'Israel'. It means in the past the chosen nation, in the present the international fellowship of believers, and in the future a growing community, including many Jews who will finally turn to the Lord.

We conclude where Paul invites us, namely to 'consider ... the kindness and sternness (or 'severity') of God' (Romans 11:22).

First, *his sternness*. The God of the biblical revelation is the God both of salvation and of judgment. Indeed, the history of Israel is a solemn warning against unfaithfulness. 'For if God did not spare the natural branches, he will not spare you either' (verse 21). So let's not provoke God.

Secondly, *his kindness*. The history of Israel, and indeed of the world, is the story of the patient loving kindness of the Lord.

> Just as you [sc. Gentiles], who were at one time disobedient to God, have now received mercy as a result of their [the Jews'] disobedience, so they too have now become disobedient in order that they too may now receive mercy as a result of God's mercy to you. For God has bound all men over to disobedience so that he may have mercy on them all.
> (Romans 11:30–32)

God's missionary purpose (his purpose of mercy) is not yet over. The faith of Jesus still has a great future, because of the mercy of God. The religions of the world may threaten the spread of the gospel. Hinduism may try to absorb Christianity, Islam to conquer it, Marxism to drive it underground, and secularism to suffocate it. But God's mercy will triumph in the end. The 'fullness' of the Jews (verse 12) and the 'fullness' of the Gentiles (verse 25) have not yet been brought in. But God is going to have mercy on the full number of all his people.

Then we will wake up to find ourselves not a tiny remnant, but a part of that vast, indeed countless, multitude of God's redeemed people gathered in from all the nations (Revelation 7:9). Only then will God's promise to Abraham be fulfilled, that his posterity will be as numerous as the stars in the sky and the sand on the seashores of the world.

Glossary

amillennialism There will be no literal or physical kingdom on earth when Christ returns. The kingdom of God is present in the world now as Christ rules the church through his Word and the Spirit. Revelation 20 is metaphorical.

apartheid A Dutch Afrikaans word derived from the root 'apart' meaning 'separate', and 'heid' meaning 'hood'. It describes the legal and institutional segregation of people on the basis of their race or colour.

apocalyptic Derived from Revelation 1:1 and meaning 'unveiling', it refers to biblical or extra-biblical literature that reveals the mystery of God's end-time purposes prior to the return of Jesus Christ.

Armageddon From the Hebrew for 'Mountain of Megiddo', it is mentioned in Revelation 16:16 as the place where the final battle on earth will take place. Others understand it as a symbol of the final overthrow of evil by God.

covenant A solemn and binding commitment between God and his people. Based on Jeremiah 31 and the New Testament, the 'new' covenant is a synonym for God's grace revealed in the redemption of Christ resulting in a church of Jews and Gentiles.

covenant theology Scripture delineates God's plan of salvation under two covenants. The promise was life, the proviso obedience, the penalty death. Under the first, Adam failed, under the second, Jesus triumphed in our place.

dispensationalism Seven periods of time during which humanity has been or will be tested according to some specific revelation of God. Israel and the church are separate. The millennium will be the culmination of God's purposes for Israel.

end times Synonymous with the 'last days' and used in Scripture to describe the period of history from the death of Christ to his return. More particularly used by premillennialists and dispensationalists to describe the present era.

eschatology From the Greek *eschatos* meaning 'last' and *logos* meaning 'word'; the doctrine of the future and specifically the events preceding the return of Christ. Variants include futurist, idealist, historicist and realized.

evangelicalism A movement within Protestant Christianity that emphasizes a personal relationship with God through Jesus Christ, a commitment to the Bible as the infallible Word of God, and the sharing of the gospel with unbelievers.

hermeneutics The Greek word *hermeneia* (meaning 'interpretation') denotes the principles used in biblical interpretation. Historically these include allegorical (Roman Catholic), typological (Reformed) and literalist (fundamentalist).

literalism The interpretation of Scripture, especially prophecy, based upon the plain meaning of the words of the text. Usually distinguished from grammatical-historical interpretation, literalism is associated most frequently with futurism.

millennium A 1,000-year reign on earth based on Revelation 20 when Satan is bound and Christ reigns on earth. Usually associated with covenantal premillennialism, dispensational premillennialism or postmillennialism.

postmillennialism An extended period of peace and prosperity on earth prior to the return of Christ. The gospel will be proclaimed to all nations and Christian values will be universally embraced. Revelation 20 is symbolic.

premillennialism A literal 1,000-year kingdom on earth following the sudden return of Christ. There are two variants, covenantal and dispensational, depending on whether Israel and the church will share eternity together.

preterism The events prophesied by Jesus prior to his death and the book of Revelation either occurred by AD 70 when Jerusalem and the temple were destroyed, or by the fall of the Roman Empire in the fifth century AD.

rapture Covenantalism teaches believers will be united with Christ when he returns. Dispensationalists divide the event into two parts. A secret rapture will remove believers during the tribulation after which they will appear with Christ.

restorationism The conviction that the Bible predicts and mandates a final and complete restoration of the Jewish people to Israel. This Christian movement preceded the rise of Jewish Zionism and facilitates Jews to make *aliyah* (return to their homeland).

typology A method of interpretation in which Old Testament 'types' are seen as fulfilled in the New Testament. These include people (David), places (Zion) and events (Passover) which are prefigurements or shadows of New Testament realities.

Zionism The national movement for the return of the Jewish people to their ancient homeland and the resumption of Jewish political sovereignty in the land of Israel centred on Jerusalem as their eternal and undivided capital.

Notes

Preface

1 Cyrus Scofield, *Scofield Reference Bible* (London: Oxford University Press, 1917).

2 Hal Lindsey, *The Late Great Planet Earth* (London: Lakeland, 1970).

3 Colin Chapman, *Whose Promised Land?* (Oxford: Lion, 2002).

4 Gary Burge, *Who Are God's People in the Middle East?* (Grand Rapids: Zondervan, 1993).

5 Grace Halsell, *Prophecy and Politics: Militant Evangelists on the Road to Nuclear War* (Westport: Lawrence Hill, 1986); *Forcing God's Hand: Why Millions Pray for a Quick Rapture . . . and Destruction of Planet Earth* (Washington: Crossroads International, 1999).

6 Donald Wagner, *Anxious for Armageddon* (Scottdale: Herald Press, 2001).

7 Stephen Sizer, *Christian Zionism: Road-map to Armageddon?* (Leicester: IVP, 2004). For some reviews, see <http://www.cc-vw.org/articles/ivp.html>. [Accessed February 2007.]

8 See <http://www.campus-watch.org>. [Accessed March 2007.]

9 See <http://www.muzzlewatch.com>. [Accessed March 2007.]

Chapter 1

1 John Hagee, The One Jerusalem Blog, 25 January 2007, <http://www.onejerusalem.org/blog/archives/2007/01/audio_exclusive_12.asp>. [Accessed March 2007.]

2 'Christians for Israel' Editorial, *The Jerusalem Post*, 14 March 2007, <http://www.jpost.com/servlet/Satellite?cid=1173879085796&pagename=JPost%2FJPArticle%2FShowFull>. [Accessed March 2007.]

3 The Pew Research Center for the People and the Press and The Pew Forum on Religion and Public Life, 'Many Americans Uneasy with Mix of Religion and Politics', 24 August 2006. The Pew Research Center for the People and the Press, <http://peoplepress.org/reports/display.php3?PageID=1084>. [Accessed March 2007.]

4 The Pew Research Center for the People and the Press, 'Americans' Support for Israel Unchanged by Recent Hostilities', 26 July 2006. The Pew Research Center, <http://pewresearch.org/pubs237/americans-support-for-israel-unchanged-by-recent-hostilities>. [Accessed June 2007.]

5 See <http://www.israelunitycoalition.org/about/index.php>. [Accessed March 2007.]

6 See Robert Jewett and John Shelton Lawrence, *Captain America and the Crusade Against Evil* (Grand Rapids: Eerdmans, 2003); Timothy Weber, *On the Road to Armageddon: How Evangelicals Became Israel's Best Friend* (Grand Rapids: Baker, 2004); and John Mearsheimer and Stephen Walt, 'The Israeli Lobby', *The London Review of Books*, 23 March 2006, <http://www.lrb.co.uk/v28/n06/mear01_.html>. [Accessed March 2007.]

7 See chapter 7 and the glossary for an explanation of these terms.

8 Vaughan Roberts, *God's Big Picture* (Leicester: IVP, 2003), p. 22.

9 C. I. Scofield, 'Introduction', *Scofield Reference Bible* (Oxford: Oxford University Press, 1917), p. 5.

10 Jimmy Carter, *Palestine: Peace not Apartheid* (New York: Simon & Schuster, 2006); Uri Davis, *Apartheid Israel* (London: Zed Books, 2003); Ilan Pappe, *The Ethnic Cleansing of Palestine* (Oxford: Oneworld, 2006).

11 Rabbi Shlomo Chaim Hacohen Aviner, cited in Grace Halsell, *Forcing God's Hand* (Washington: Crossroads International, 1999), p. 71.

12 Yisrael Meida, cited in Halsell, *Forcing God's Hand*, p. 68.

Chapter 2

1 Two books well worth considering if you want to learn how to study the Bible are: Nigel Beynon and Andrew Sach, *Dig Deeper* (Leicester: IVP, 2005) and Jan Johnson, *Study and Meditation* (Leicester: IVP, 2003).

2   Alec Motyer, 'Bible Study and the Unity of the Bible' in John B. Job (ed.), *Studying God's Word* (London: IVP, 1972), p. 14.

3   See, for example, the *New Bible Commentary: 21st Century Edition*, ed. D. A. Carson, R. T. France, J. A. Motyer and G. J. Wenham (Leicester: IVP, 1994).

4   A good website to look at for further Bible study is <www.bible.org>.

5   C. I. Scofield, *Scofield Bible Correspondence Course*, 9th edn (Chicago: Moody Bible Institute, 1907), pp. 45–46.

6   Motyer, 'Bible Study and the Unity of the Bible', p. 15.

7   Edgar C. Whisenant, *88 Reasons Why the Rapture Will Be in 1988* (Nashville: World Bible Society, 1988).

8   Edgar C. Whisenant, *The Final Shout: Rapture Report 1989* (Nashville: World Bible Society, 1989).

9   C. Marvin Pate and Calvin B. Haines Jr, *Doomsday Delusions* (Downers Grove: IVP, 1995).

10 Adapted from J. Barton Payne, *Encyclopedia of Biblical Prophecy* (Grand Rapids: Baker, 1980), pp. 86–87.

11 Adapted from C. Marvin Pate and Calvin B. Haines Jr, *Doomsday Delusions*, p. 24. See also Leon Morris, *Apocalyptic* (Leicester: IVP, 1972), pp. 34–61.

12 Pate and Haines, *Doomsday Delusions*, p. 28.

13 Michael Wilcock, *I Saw Heaven Opened: The Message of Revelation* (Leicester: IVP, 1975), p. 24.

14 William Hendriksen, *More than Conquerors: An Interpretation of the Book of Revelation* (London: IVP, 1940), p. 49.

15 Wilcock, *I Saw Heaven Opened*, p. 23.

16 Hal Lindsey, *The Late Great Planet Earth* (London: Lakeland, 1970), p. 160.

17 Hal Lindsey, 'Uncovered: Russian-Syrian-Iranian Axis', *Oracle Commentaries* (22 July 2006), <http://www.hallindseyoracle.com/articles.asp?ArticleID=13165>. [Accessed August 2006.]

18 Hal Lindsey, *The 1980's: Countdown to Armageddon* (New York: Bantam, 1981), p. 68.

19 Hal Lindsey, *Planet Earth 2000 AD* (Palos Verdes, CA: Western Front, 1994), p. 216.

20 Charles H. Dyer, *The Rise of Babylon: Sign of the End Times* (Wheaton: Tyndale, 1991).

21 Charles H. Dyer, *What's Next? God, Israel and the Bible* (Chicago: Moody, 2004).

22 Hal Lindsey, *Israel and the Last Days* (Eugene, Oregon: Harvest House, 1983), pp. 32–33.

23 Hal Lindsey, *Apocalypse Code* (Palos Verdes, CA: Western Front, 1997), pp. 42, 47.

24 M. R. DeHann, *Revelation: 35 Simple Studies in the Major Themes of Revelation* (Grand Rapids: Zondervan, 1946), p. 148.

25 Hal Lindsey, *There's a New World Coming: A Prophetic Odyssey* (Santa Ana, CA: Vision House, 1973); pp. 142–143.

26 Tim LaHaye and Jerry Jenkins, *Are We Living in the End Times?* (Wheaton: Tyndale House, 1999), pp. 190–192.

27 Schuyler English (ed.), *The New Scofield Reference Bible* (New York: Oxford University Press, 1984), p. 143.

28 Lindsey, *New World Coming*, p. 143.

29 William Hendrikson, *More than Conquerors: An Interpretation of the Book of Revelation* (London: IVP, 1973), pp. 40–41.

30 Lindsey, *Apocalypse Code*, p. 78.

31 Lindsey, *Planet Earth 2000 A D* , pp. 182–183.

32 C. I. Scofield, *Scofield Reference Bible* (London: Oxford University Press, 1917), p. 883.

33 Grant Jeffrey, *Messiah: War in the Middle East & the Road to Armageddon* (Toronto: Frontier Research Publications, 1991), pp. 98ff.

34 LaHaye and Jenkins, *Are We Living in the End Times?*, p. 86.

35 Edwin Yamauchi, *Foes from the Northern Frontier* (Grand Rapids: Baker, 1982), pp. 19–27; Ralph H. Alexander, *Ezekiel: The Expositor's Bible Commentary* (Grand Rapids, Michigan: Zondervan, 1986), p. 930.

36 John B. Taylor, *Ezekiel: Tyndale Old Testament Commentary* (London: IVP, 1969), pp. 243–246.

37 Noah Hutchings, *U.S. in Prophecy* (Oklahoma City: Hearthstone Publishing, 2000); Mark Hitchcock, *Is America in Prophecy?* (Portland, Oregon: Multnomah, 2002); Hal Lindsey, *Where is America in Prophecy?* video (Murrieta, CA: Hal Lindsey Ministries, 2001).

38 Lindsey, *New World Coming*, p. 185.

39 Mike D. Evans, *The American Prophecies: Ancient Scriptures Reveal our Nation's Future* (New York: Warner, 2004), pp. 5–7.

40 Gail Hudson, Editorial Review, Amazon, <http://www.amazon.com/gp/product/044652252X/103–5325893–4368626?v=glance&n=283155>. [Accessed August 2006.]

41 Evans, *American Prophecies*, p. 26.

42 D. S. Russell, *Apocalyptic: Ancient and Modern* (Philadelphia: Fortress, 1987), p. 64. See also by the same author, *Prophecy and the Ancient Dream* (Peabody: Hendrickson, 1994).

Chapter 3

1 Cited in Grace Halsell, *Forcing God's Hand* (Washington: Crossroads International, 1999), p. 100.

2 Dennis Prager, 'Those Who Curse the Jews and Those Who Bless the Jews', Christian Action for Israel, <http://christianactionforisrael.org/antiholo/curse.html>. [Accessed August 2006.]

3 Christians United for Israel, Long Term Goals, <http://www.cufi.org/information.aspx>. [Accessed August 2006.]

4 C. I. Scofield, *Rightly Dividing the Word of Truth*, (New York: Loizeaux Brothers, 1896), p. 3.

5 Lewis Sperry Chafer, *Dispensationalism* (Dallas: Seminary Press, 1936), p. 107; *Systematic Theology* (Dallas: Dallas Seminary Press, 1975), vol. 4. pp. 315–323.

6 John Hagee, *Final Dawn over Jerusalem* (Nashville: Thomas Nelson, 1998), pp. 108–109.

7 Christian Friends of Israel, *About Us*, <https://www.cfi.org.uk/aboutus.php>. [Accessed August 2006.]

8 Jews for Jesus, *Our Doctrinal Statement*, <http://www.jfjonline.org/about/statementoffaith.htm>. [Accessed August 2006.]

9 David Brickner, *Future Hope* (San Francisco: Purpose Pomegranate, 1999), p. 18.

10 Gilbert Bilezikian, unpublished correspondence, August 2006.

11 The International Christian Embassy, Jerusalem: Get Involved. <http://www.icej.org/article/get_involved>. [Accessed August 2006.]

12 *International Christian Zionist Congress Proclamation*, The International Christian Embassy, Jerusalem, 25–29 February 1996. <http://christianactionforisrael.org/congress.html>. [Accessed August 2006.]

13 Hal Lindsey, Urgent Personal Message, 30 November 2005, <www.hallindseyoracle.com/articles.asp?ArticleID=12130>. [Accessed August 2006.]

14 C. I. Scofield, *Scofield Reference Bible* (Oxford: Oxford University Press, 1917), fn. 1, p. 25.

15 E. Schuyler English, *The New Scofield Study Bible* (New York: Oxford University Press, 1984), p. 18.

16 On one other occasion in the Old Testament, a similar blessing is given by Balaam on the Israelites as they wandered in the wilderness, 'May those who bless you be blessed and those who curse you be cursed!' (Numbers 24:9).

17 *Scofield Reference Bible*, fn. 1, p. 1036.

18 Schuyler English, *The New Scofield Study Bible*, fn. 3, pp. 1012–1013.

19 John Stott, *Only One way: The Message of Galatians* (London: IVP, 1968), p. 180.

20 Ibid., p. 181.

21 Bruce Milne, *The Message of John* (Leicester: IVP, 1993), p. 219.

22 Ibid., p. 219.

23 *Scofield Reference Bible*, fn. 1, p. 1206.

24 Arnold Fruchtenbaum, *Israelology: The Missing Link in Systematic Theology* (Tustin, California: Ariel Ministries, 1989), p. 552; John Walvoord, *The Millennial Kingdom* (Grand Rapids: Dunham publishing, 1958), pp. 190–192; Lewis Sperry Chafer, *Systematic Theology*, 8 vols. (Dallas: Dallas Seminary Press, 1947), vol. 3, pp. 105–108.

25 O. Palmer Robertson, *The Israel of God* (Phillipsburg, New Jersey: Presbyterian & Reformed, 2000), pp. 180–192.

26 Martyn Lloyd-Jones, *The Church and the Last Things* (London: Hodder & Stoughton, 2002), p. 113.

27 Louis Berkhof, *Systematic Theology* (Grand Rapids: Eerdmans, 1939), pp. 698–700.

28 John Stott, *The Message of Romans* (Leicester: IVP, 1994), p. 303.

29 F. F. Bruce, *The Letter of Paul to the Romans* (Leicester: IVP, 1963), p. 209, cited in Stott, *Message of Romans*. This view is also shared by Iain Murray, *The Puritan Hope* (Edinburgh: Banner of Truth, 1971).

30 Steve Motyer, *Israel in the Plan of God* (Leicester: IVP, 1989), pp. 151, 157.

31 Leon Morris, *The Epistle to the Romans* (Grand Rapids: Eerdmans, 1988), pp. 420–421.

32 John Calvin, *The Epistle of Paul the Apostle to the Romans* (Edinburgh: St Andrew Press, 1961), p. 255.

33 O. Palmer Robertson, *Israel of God*, p. 188.

34 Ibid., p. 188.

Chapter 4

1 David Brickner, 'What do we think about modern Israel?' Jews for
   Jesus Prayer Letter, April 1998, <http://www.new-life.net/israel.htm>.
   [Accessed August 2006.]

2 International Christian Zionist Congress Proclamation, The International
   Christian Embassy, Jerusalem, 25–29 February 1996. <http://
   christianactionforisrael.org/congress.html>. [Accessed August
   2006.]

3 C. I. Scofield, *Scofield Reference Bible* (Oxford: Oxford University Press,
   1909), p. 250.

4 Arnold Fruchtenbaum, 'The Land is Mine', *Issues*, 2.4, July 1982,
   <http://www.jewsforjesus.org/publications/issues/2_4/land>.
   [Accessed August 2006.]

5 Patrick Goodenough, Letter from the International Christian Embassy
   to Christian Peacemaker Teams, 31 October 1997, 'Blessing Israel?
   Christian Embassy Responds, Kern Replies', <http://www.cpt.org/
   archives/1997/nov97/0000.html>. [Accessed August 2006.]

6 Exobus, <http://www.exobus.org>. [Accessed August 2006.]

7 Christian Friends of Israeli Communities, <http://www.cfoic.com>.
   [Accessed August 2006.]

8 *Scofield Reference Bible*, note, p. 25.

9 E. Schuyler English, *The Scofield Study Bible*, rev. edn (New York:
   Oxford University Press, 1967), p. 293.

10 E. Schuyler English, *The New Scofield Study Bible* (New York: Oxford
    University Press, 1984), p. 217.

11 Hal Lindsey, *The Road to Holocaust* (New York: Bantam, 1989), p. 180.

12 Charles H. Spurgeon, *Lectures to My Students* (London: Passmore &
    Alabaster, 1893), p. 100.

13 Charles H. Spurgeon, *Lectures to My Students*, First Series (London:
    Passmore & Alabaster, 1877), p. 83.

14 John Calvin, *The Acts of the Apostles 1 – 13* (Edinburgh: St Andrew Press,
    1965), p. 29.

15 John R. W. Stott, *The Message of Acts* (Leicester: IVP, 1990), pp. 40–41.

16 Hal Lindsey, *The Late Great Planet Earth* (London: Lakeland, 1970),
    p. 53.

17 *Scofield Reference Bible*, fn. 1, pp. 1169–1170.

18 Ibid., fn. 1, p. 1170.

19 Stott, *Message of Acts*, p. 43.

Chapter 5

1 Nelson Bell, editorial, *Christianity Today*, 21 July 1967, p. 28.

2 'Prophets in Jerusalem', *Newsweek*, 28 June 1971, p. 62.

3 'International Christian Zionist Congress Proclamation', International Christian Embassy, Jerusalem, 25–29 February 1996.

4 'Christians Call for a United Jerusalem', *New York Times*, 18 April 1997, <http://www.cdn-friends-icej.ca/united.html>. [Accessed June 2007.]

5 Ibid.

6 Mike Evans, 'Israel does not exist!', <www.freeman.org/m_online/apr04/evans.htm>. [Accessed June 2007.]

7 John Hagee, *Jerusalem Betrayed* (Dallas: Word, 1997), p. 42.

8 The Jerusalem Summit, 'The Jerusalem Declaration', <http://www.jerusalemsummit.org/eng/declaration_full.php>. [Accessed March 2007.]

9 Peter Walker, 'Jerusalem' in T. Desmond Alexander and Brian S. Rosner (eds.), *New Dictionary of Biblical Theology* (Leicester: IVP, 2000), p. 589.

10 Hal Lindsey, *Israel and the Last Days* (Eugene, Oregon: Harvest House, 1983), p. 20.

11 Hal Lindsey, *Planet Earth 2000 AD: Will Mankind Survive?* (Palos Verdes, California: Western Front, 1994), p. 247.

12 Cyrus Scofield, *Scofield Reference Bible* (New York: Oxford University Press, 1917), fn. 1, p. 883.

13 Ibid., p. 262.

14 Lindsey, *Israel and the Last Days*, p. 165.

15 Colin Chapman, *Whose Holy City?* (Oxford: Lion, 2004), p. 30.

16 Lindsey, *Planet Earth 2000 AD*, p. 164.

17 Hal Lindsey, *The Final Battle* (Palos Verdes, California: Western Front, 1995), p. 95.

18 Mike Evans, *Jerusalem Betrayed: Ancient Prophecy and Modern Conspiracy Collide in the Holy City* (Dallas: Word, 1997), p. 193.

19 *Scofield Reference Bible*, fn. 2, p. 1106.

20 E. Schuyler English, *The New Scofield Study Bible* (New York: Oxford University Press, 1984), p. 1084. Schuyler English does the same thing in a footnote to Revelation 16:19.

21 Kenneth Barker (ed.), *Today's New International Study Bible* (Grand Rapids: Zondervan, 2006), p. 2133.

22 Peter Walker, *Jesus and the Holy City* (Grand Rapids: Eerdmans, 1996), p. 101.

23 Norval Geldenhuys, *Commentary on the Gospel of Luke* (London: Marshall, Morgan and Scott, 1950), p. 528.

24 Chapman, *Whose Holy City?*, p. 39.

25 Walker, *Jesus and the Holy City*, p. 102.

26 Ibid., p. 131.

27 J. C. De Young, *Jerusalem in the New Testament* (Amsterdam: J. H. Kok/ N. V. Kampen, 1961), p. 106. Cited in Walker, *Jesus and the Holy City*, p. 131.

28 Walker, *Jesus and the Holy City*, p. 320.

29 Peter Walker, 'Jesus and Jerusalem: New Testament Perspectives' in Naim Ateek, Cedar Duaybis and Maria Schrader (eds.), *Jerusalem: What Makes for Peace!* (London: Melesende, 1997), pp. 62, 66, 67.

Chapter 6

1 Hal Lindsey, 'World's Fate Hangs on 35 Acres', *World Net Daily*, 21 February 2001, <http://www.wnd.com/news/ article.asp?ARTICLE_ID=21794>. [Accessed August 2006.]

2 Kara G. Morrison, 'Believers, breeder await sacred cow: How a Pentecostal minister, an Orthodox rabbi and a Catholic cattle rancher started raising holy heifers', The American Association of Sunday and Feature Editors (AASFE), <http://www.aasfe.org/kara-morrison-2.html>. [Accessed June 2007.]

3 Christians United for Israel, <http://www.cufi.org>. [Accessed March 2007.]

4 John Hubers, 'The Christian Zionist Fantasyland', <http:// www.christianzionism.org>. [Accessed March 2007.]

5 John Hagee, *The Battle for Jerusalem* (Nashville: Thomas Nelson, 2001).

6 Richard N. Ostling, 'Time for a New Temple?', *Time* (16 October 1989), p. 64.

7 Randall Price, *The Coming Last Days Temple* (Eugene, Oregon: Harvest House, 1999), p. 26.

8 Firas Al-Atraqchi, 'Jewish groups: Raze mosques, rebuild Temple', Al Jazeera, 28 July 2004, <http://english.aljazeera.net/NR/exeres/58087655–FE76–4764–9598–A952E08FEFC8.htm>. [Accessed August 2006.]

9 Yizhar Be'er, 'Targeting the Temple Mount: A Current Look at Threats to the Temple Mount by Extremist and Messianic Groups',

Keshev, <http://keshev.org.il/siteEn/FullNews.asp?NewsID= 53&CategoryID=14>. [Accessed August 2006.]

10 Gershon Salomon, *The Voice of the Temple Mount Faithful*, 5761/2001, pp. 15–17.

11 N. Shragai, 'Rabbis call for mass visits to Temple Mount', *Ha'aretz*, 19 July 2001.

12 Hal Lindsey, *The Late Great Planet Earth* (London: Lakeland, 1970), pp. 56–58.

13 Randall Price, 'Time for a Temple? Jewish Plans to Rebuild the Temple', *Israel My Glory*, January 1998, Friends of Israel Gospel Ministry, <http://www.apocalypsesoon.org/xfile-4.html>. [Accessed August 2006.]

14 Zhava Glaser, 'Today's Rituals: Reminders or Replacements?', May 1992, Jews for Jesus, <www.jewsforjesus.org/publications/issues/8_3/ rituals>. [Accessed August 2006.]

15 International Christian Embassy, 'About the Feast of Tabernacles', <www.icej.org/articles/about_the_feast> and the International Christian Zionist Centre, <www.israelmybeloved.com/channel/ tabernacles>. [Accessed August 2006.]

16 C. I. Scofield, *Scofield Reference Bible* (New York: Oxford University Press, 1945), p. 890.

17 E. Schuyler English (ed.), *The New Scofield Study Bible* (New York: Oxford University Press, 1984), p. 864.

18 David Brickner, *Future Hope* (San Francisco: Purpose Pomegranate, 1999), p. 18.

19 Hal Lindsey, *Apocalypse Code* (Palos Verdes, California: Western Front, 1997), p. 78.

20 See Flavius Josephus, 'Jewish Antiquities', in *The New Complete Works of Josephus* (Grand Rapids: Kregel, 1999).

21 See <www.armageddonbooks.com/309hal.html>. [Accessed August 2006.]

22 Hal Lindsey, *Planet Earth 2000* (Palos Verde, California: Western Front, 1994), pp. 156, 163.

23 Grace Halsell, *Forcing God's Hand* (Washington: Crossroads International, 1999), pp. 68–69.

24 Randall Price, *The Coming Last Days Temple* (Eugene, OR: Harvest House, 2002).

25 Charles Colson, *Kingdoms in Conflict* (London: Hodder, 1988), prologue.

26 Palestine Media Centre, 'Jewish Extremists of Temple Mount Faithful to Enter Al-Aqsa Thursday', 2 August 2006, <http://www.palestine-pmc.com/alerts/2-8-06.asp>. [Accessed August 2006.]

27 Sam Kiley, 'The righteous will survive and the rest will perish', *The Times*, 13 December 1999, p. 39.

28 Halsell, *Forcing God's Hand*, p. 71.

29 Cited in Grace Halsell, *Prophecy and Politics: The Secret Alliance Between Israel and the U.S. Christian Right* (Chicago: Lawrence Hill Books, 1986), p. 115.

30 Lawrence Wright, 'Letter from Jerusalem: Forcing the End', *New Yorker*, 20 July 1998, <www.lawrencewright.com/art-jerusalem.html>. [Accessed August 2006.]

Chapter 7

1 Tim Lahaye's *Left Behind* collection includes eight volumes in the adult series and twenty-four volumes in the children's edition, as well as videos and the DVD game. Total sales exceed 60 million copies. <www.leftbehind.com>. [Accessed January 2007.]

2 See Stephen Sizer, *Christian Zionism: Road-map to Armageddon?* (Leicester: IVP, 2004), pp. 191–202; J. N. Darby, 'The Rapture of the Saints and the Character of the Jewish Remnant', *Collected Writings*, vol. 2, Prophetic 1, pp. 153–155.

3 Hal Lindsey, *The Late Great Planet Earth* (London: Lakeland, 1970), p. 136.

4 See <http://www.raptureready.com/rr-secret-rapture.html>. [Accessed January 2007.]

5 John Walvoord, *End Times: Understanding Today's World Events in Biblical Prophecy* (Waco, Texas: Word, 1998); Jews for Jesus, <http://www.store.jewsforjesus.org/books/products/BK232.htm>. [Accessed June 2004.]

6 Jews for Jesus, <http://www.store.jewsforjesus.org/books/products/sp057.htm>.

7 Cyrus Scofield, *Scofield Reference Bible* (Oxford: Oxford University Press, 1945), fn. 1, p. 1016.

8 Ibid., fn. 1, p. 1148.

9 J. N. Darby, *Synopsis of the Books of the Bible*, vol. 5. (London: G. Morrish, n.d.), p. 91.

10 J. N. Darby, *Collected Writings*, vol. 2, Prophetic 4, p. 118.

11 Hal Lindsey, *Planet Earth 2000 A D* (Palos Verdes: Western Front, 1994), p. 29.

12 For useful critiques of the two-stage rapture theory, see Crawford Gribben, *Rapture Fiction and the Evangelical Crisis* (Webster, New York: Evangelical Press, 2006); and Dave MacPherson, *The Great Rapture Hoax* (Fletcher, North Carolina: New Puritan Library, 1983).

13 See Ted Noel, *I Want to be Left Behind* (Maitland, Florida: Bible Only Press, 2002).

14 Brian Braiker, 'Are These the End Times?', *Newsweek*, 28 July 2006, <http://www.msnbc.msn.com/id/14083809/site/newsweek>. [Accessed January 2007.]

15 See <http://www.raptureready.com>. [Accessed January 2007.]

16 See <www.raptureready.com>. [Accessed November 2006.]

17 *Scofield Reference Bible*, fn. 4, pp. 1348–1349.

18 Charles Ryrie, *The Living End* (Old Tappan: Revell, 1976), p. 81. Chapter 8 is entitled 'A Bloodbath for Israel'.

19 John Walvoord, *Israel in Prophecy* (Grand Rapids: Zondervan), p. 108.

20 Tim LaHaye and Jerry Jenkins, *Are we Living in the End Times?* (Wheaton, IL: Tyndale House, 2000), p. 146.

21 Hal Lindsey, *The Final Battle* (Palos Verdes, CA: Western Front, 1995), p. 184.

22 Ibid., pp. 255–257.

23 Sarah Posner, 'Pastor Strangelove', The American Prospect Online, <http://www.prospect.org/web/page.ww?section=root&name=ViewPrint&articleId=11541>. [Accessed March 2007.]

24 Lindsey, *Final Battle*, pp. 251–252, 284.

25 William Hendriksen, *More than Conquerors* (London, IVP: 1940), p. 156.

26 See Stanley J. Grenz, *The Millennial Maze: Sorting out Evangelical Options* (Downers Grove: InterVarsity Press, 1992); Robert G. Clouse (ed.), *The Meaning of the Millennium* (Downers Grove: InterVarsity Press, 1977); Steve Gregg (ed.), *Revelation: Four Views – A Parallel Commentary* (Nashville: Thomas Nelson, 1997).

27 The illustrations for the three main views of the millennium are adapted from Wayne Grudem, *Systematic Theology* (Leicester: IVP, 1994), pp. 1109–1111.

28 Grace Halsell, *Prophecy and Politics: Militant Evangelicals on the Road to Nuclear War* (Westport: Lawrence Hill, 1986), p. 195; see also Gary

DeMar and Peter Leithart, *The Legacy of Hatred Continues* (Tyler, TX: Institute of Christian Economics, 1989), p. 26.

29 R. C. Sproul, *The Last Days According to Jesus* (Grand Rapids: Baker, 1998); see also <http://www.preterist.org> and <http://www.preterism.com>.

30 Gary DeMar, *Last Days Madness* (Atlanta: American Vision, 1997).

31 John Noe, *Beyond the End Times* (Bradford: International Preterist Association, 1999).

32 Max King, *The Spirit of Prophecy* (Colorado Springs: Bimillennial Press, 2000). 'Transmillennial' and 'Transmillennialism' are trademarks of the Council on Transmillennialism, <http://www.transmillennial.com>. [Accessed July 2007.]

Chapter 8

1 Vaughan Roberts, *God's Big Picture: Tracing the Story-line of the Bible* (Leicester: IVP, 2003), p. 149.

2 Ibid., p. 21.

3 Graeme Goldsworthy, *Gospel and Kingdom* (Exeter: Paternoster, 1981), p. 47.

4 Craig L. Blomberg, *From Pentecost to Patmos: Acts to Revelation. An Introduction and Survey* (Nottingham: Apollos, 2006), p. 419.

5 David Breese, *Know the Marks of the Cults* (Eastbourne: Victor Books, 1975), p. 11.

6 Graeme Goldsworthy, *According to Plan: The Unfolding Revelation of God in the Bible* (Leicester: IVP, 1991), p. 63.

7 Blomberg, *From Pentecost to Patmos*, p. 37.

8 David J. Bosch, *Transforming Mission: Paradigm Shifts in Theology of Mission* (Maryknoll: Orbis, 2000), p. 141.

Recommended further reading

1. How to read the Bible

Nigel Beynon and Andrew Sach, *Dig Deeper* (Leicester: IVP, 2005)

Graeme Goldsworthy, *Gospel-Centred Hermeneutics* (Notttingham: Apollos, 2006)

Jan Johnson, *Study and Meditation* (Leicester: IVP, 2003)

2. Israel and the church

David Holwerda, *Jesus and Israel: One Covenant or Two?* (Leicester: Apollos, 1995)

Stephen Motyer, *Israel in the Plan of God* (Leicester: IVP, 1989)

O. Palmer Robertson, *The Israel of God* (Phillipsburg, NJ: Presbyterian & Reformed, 2000)

3. The Promised Land

Gary Burge, *Whose Land? Whose Promise?* (Carlisle: Paternoster, 2003)

Colin Chapman, *Whose Promised Land? The Continuing Crisis over Israel and Palestine* (Oxford: Lion, 2002)

Philip Johnston and Peter Walker (eds.), *The Land of Promise* (Leicester: Apollos, 2000)

4. The battle for Jerusalem

Colin Chapman, *Whose Holy City?* (Oxford: Lion, 2004)

Peter W. L. Walker, *Jesus and the Holy City: New Testament Perspectives on Jerusalem* (Grand Rapids: Eerdmans, 1996)

Peter W. L. Walker (ed.), *Jerusalem: Past and Present in the Purposes of God* (Carlisle: Paternoster, 1994)

5. The role of the temple

T. D. Alexander and S. Gathercole (eds.), *Heaven on Earth: The Temple in Biblical Theology* (Carlisle: Paternoster, 2004)

G. K. Beale, *The Temple and the Church's Mission: A Biblical Theology of the Dwelling Place of God* (Leicester: Apollos, 2004)

Alfred Edersheim, *The Temple: Its Ministry and Services* (Peabody: Hendrickson, 1994)

6. How to understand the future

Hank Hanegraaff, *The Apocalypse Code* (Nashville: Nelson, 2007)

R. C. Sproul, *The Last Days According to Jesus* (Grand Rapids: Baker, 2000)

Cornelis P. Venema, *The Promise of the Future* (Edinburgh: Banner of Truth, 2000)

7. Christian Zionism

Naim Ateek (ed.), *Challenging Christian Zionism* (London: Melisende, 2005)

Stephen Sizer, *Christian Zionism: Road-map to Armageddon?* (Leicester: IVP, 2004)

Timothy Weber, *On the Road to Armageddon: How Evangelicals Became Israel's Best Friend* (Grand Rapids: Baker, 2004)

Index of biblical references